JUNIOR
SOCCER

hamlyn

JUNIOR
SOCCER

ADAM WARD
& TREVOR LEWIN

ACKNOWLEDGEMENTS

The authors would like to thank the following people for their help at various stages of this project: Trevor Davies and Camilla James at Hamlyn; Peter Stewart at West Ham United; Joe Ward and Ben Lewin for demonstrating their extraordinary footballing skills; Fila UK for providing the kit for the photoshoot; Nick Wright and Mark Newcombe for their good humour, patience and camera skills; parents and players for the time they gave up so willingly during their precious summer holiday to attend the shoot; and Martin Topping for his design skills. Particular thanks must also go to Jim Hampsheir for his good humour and excellent coaching.

PUBLISHER'S NOTES

Gender – On the majority of occasions players have been referred to as 'he' in the book. This is simply for convenience and in no way reflects an opinion that soccer is a male-only sport.

Safety and Equipment – Coaches should take care to follow manufacturers' instructions when setting up any training equipment. In particular, portable goals should always be properly erected and anchored firmly to the ground.

Shinpads – Some pictures in this book show players without shinpads. However, it is recommended that pads be worn in all practice and match situations.

Physical exertion – Coaches should be aware that, contrary to traditional wisdom, players can be worked too hard. Prolonged sessions, particulary those involving plyometric exercises, should be kept short and tailored to meet the needs and abilities of the players.

Executive Editor: **Trevor Davies**
Project Editor: **Camilla James**
Executive Art Editor: **Geoff Fennell**
Design: **Martin Topping**
Illustration: **Andy Chapman, Martin Topping**
Picture Research: **Jennifer Veall**
Production Controller: **Edward Carter**
Additional Soccer Coaching: **Jim Hampsheir**

All kit supplied by Fila (UK) Limited

First published in Great Britain in 2002
by Hamlyn, a division of Octopus Publishing Group Limited
2–4 Heron Quays, London E14 2JP

Copyright © 2002 Octopus Publishing Group Limited

ISBN 0 600 60424 1

A catalogue record for this book is available from the British Library

Printed in China

10 9 8 7 6 5 4 3 2 1

FOREWORD

The last ten years have seen soccer undergo massive changes at all levels. In my position as West Ham United's Academy Director I have been well placed to observe these changes at close quarters and, in particular, the effects they have had on the junior game. Today, there is more media interest in soccer than ever before and, as a result, there is now more pressure on young players to succeed. For example, when future England internationals Paul Ince and Tony Cottee emerged from the Hammers youth team in the 1980s there was nothing like the media interest that recently surrounded the likes of Joe Cole, Michael Carrick and Rio Ferdinand.

The pressure placed on Joe, Rio and Michael, who have been forced to grow up under intense media scrutiny, filters right down to the grass roots of the game. Parents, teachers and amateur coaches can all fall into the trap of pushing players too hard at too young an age. There is a mistaken belief that they will get the best out of children by filling their heads with tactics and complex ideas about the game. All coaches, but particularly those working with age groups up to under-12s, should keep in mind that it is possible to overcoach children.

A good coach will structure an exercise while leaving the youngsters free to play. It is important that players develop good habits and learn that improvement only comes with practice, but they must also discover things for themselves and work out their own strengths and weaknesses. Similarly, coaches must avoid pigeonholing players into positions too early.

If training is too regimented, players will never come to take responsibility for their own actions on the pitch and they will struggle to think independently during a game. The one quality that all top players share is an awareness of space and an appreciation of players around them, and this simply cannot be taught through regimented and dictatorial coaching.

Despite this reservation about the potential overcoaching of young players, it must be said that the overall standard of the junior game has improved in recent times. The soccer authorities and professional clubs have made a huge investment in the junior game, which is still ongoing, and young players are now joining professional clubs better equipped to deal with the physical and technical demands placed upon them.

At West Ham United, we have always taken pride in our youth set-up, which, after all, produced the likes of Bobby Moore, Geoff Hurst, Martin Peters and Trevor Brooking in the 1950s and 1960s, and more recently Joe Cole, Michael Carrick, Rio Ferdinand and Jermain Defoe. The emergence of the recent crop of young England players at Upton Park pays testimony to the hard work and attitude of all the coaching and scouting staff at the club. It is also fair to say that, in most cases, a solid foundation of good habits and sound technique was in place before these players arrived ... and that is down to the hard work of amateur coaches, parents and teachers. Who knows? This book may help you provide similar foundations for the youngsters under your charge.

TONY CARR, WEST HAM UNITED ACADEMY DIRECTOR

INTRODUCTION

No sport in the world evokes greater passion among its followers than soccer. Unfortunately, such extremes of emotion are not always conducive to learning the game, and junior players can often be discouraged by coaches and parents who place too much pressure on their young shoulders. The priority for anybody teaching children to play soccer is to create a learning environment that is not too intense and which enables players to develop at their own rate. This book aims to provide a framework around which an appropriate programme of instruction can be created. However, it should be remembered that the attitude and interpersonal skills of the coach will ultimately determine whether sessions are successful or not.

Coaches who shout in an aggressive manner, continually repeat instructions and persist with over-complicated drills, will invariably only succeed in alienating their players. Like any good teacher, the soccer coach should aim to make each exercise appear new and fresh, thereby building on a child's enthusiasm for the game. Instructions should be given clearly at the start of any drill, and feedback after each session should be constructive rather than overly critical.

When working with younger players (up to and around the age of seven) soccer coaches should primarily be aiming to make sessions fun, focussing on ball familiarity while fostering the child's own passion for the game. As players get older, the coach must work on more complex aspects of play and will have to explain tactical responsibilities. It is essential, however, to retain a balance between striving to improve the knowledge and skills of a group of players, and ensuring that they still retain their passion and enthusiasm for the game.

It should always be remembered that the great majority of junior players will never progress to any higher standard than Sunday morning park soccer, so the emphasis should be on enjoyment of the game. Junior soccer, it must be stressed, is about the players, and is not an opportunity for coaches to show off their tactical knowledge or for parents to live out their own dreams and ambitions through their children. If, however, you let youngsters enjoy their game and progress at their own speed, you may just find that they share not only your passion but also your aspirations.

COMMON PITFALLS

There are several common problems that afflict the junior soccer coach ... but all can be avoided with a little thought.
• Repeated instructions. By repeating the same words and phrases at a confused child, your instructions will not become any clearer. Try asking questions instead, i.e. 'Why do you think the ball keeps flying over the crossbar?', rather than just shouting 'Keep it down!' at every player.
• Avoid complicated instructions. If a drill takes longer to explain than it does to practise, it is not going to work. Explain the purpose of the exercise and offer players the chance to ask questions if they are unsure.
• Never persist with an exercise that is failing. If things are going wrong and chaos is prevailing, it is always best to call a halt to proceedings. You may lose your authority and the respect of the players if you continue with a drill that has descended into disorder. Far better to stop, move on to another exercise and go back to the drawing board.
• Do not delude yourself. You are not managing Brazil, France or Juventus. Junior soccer is not the place to prove yourself a tactical genius. Your job is to ensure that children enjoy playing the game.
• Never lose your passion for the game. Enthusiasm is infectious and it will bring out the best in your players.

GETTING STARTED

It would be wrong to suggest that a toddler's first attempt to kick a ball is of profound importance to their soccer future, but this does not mean that a child's early experiences of the game are insignificant. From the age of four, children can begin to learn how to run properly, how to position their bodies to meet a moving ball, how a bouncing or rolling ball reacts and, most importantly, they can develop an opinion about the game. Parents, teachers and coaches will all determine whether that opinion is positive or negative.

BALL FAMILIARITY

Patience is an essential quality for any sports coach, but it is particularly important to those working with junior soccer players. Contrary to what some traditionalists may believe, kicking a ball is not the first thing you should try to teach an aspiring player. Children must first become familiar with the ball, while also developing their movement and coordination. Once the child has mastered these skills, then he or she can begin to learn the art of kicking a ball properly.

It is important that youngsters grasp the fundamentals, as by doing so they will develop a solid sporting foundation that is relevant to almost any ball sport. Learning how a bouncing ball reacts, and how to position one's body to control it, is a transferable skill that will benefit tennis and basketball players as much as soccer players.

However, while movement and coordination are the priority, it is important not to deny children all contact with a soccer ball. It is essential that youngsters retain their enthusiasm for the game, and contact with a ball can help do this. The inclusion of a ball, wherever possible, will also avoid boredom and the resultant problems of waning interest.

BAD PARENT

It is easy to put pressure on young children when teaching them to play soccer. Parents must avoid the temptation of pushing their children too hard, as they are likely to alienate them from the game for good.

1 Throwing a heavy ball at a child is only likely to succeed in terrifying the youngster and will do nothing for their coordination.

2 If a child is not interested in playing with the ball, there is no point in pushing him or her. The situation will quickly become tense and the potential for successful learning will be minimal.

FIRST STEPS

Some small children respond well to having a ball thrown at them, but most do not. And the accompanying shout of 'kick it back to me', seldom brings the desired result. Each weekend, parks and playing fields are littered with parents who stand shouting ever louder at their children, demanding that they 'kick the ball'. Their efforts are rarely productive.

A better approach is for parents to provide the opportunity for their children to play with a ball while offering gentle encouragement. Most youngsters react badly to pressure, so let them dictate the speed of progress. Start with a small ball (a size-1 skills ball is ideal), and encourage the child to roll it to you at first. As they grow in confidence, they can begin throwing and even kicking the ball. Try to make this exercise fun, and avoid the temptation to prolong the session. Always end on a positive note – it is a mistake to keep going to the point of failure. Your aim is to build on the child's interest and passion for football while teaching them ball familiarity.

DO

- Use a small ball
- Focus on achievements not failure
- Start with simple throwing exercises

DO NOT

- Shout
- Repeat instructions without explanation
- Spend money on expensive football boots

GOOD PARENT

With patience and a relaxed attitude, it is possible to improve almost any child's ball skills.

1 By getting down low and rolling the ball gently along the ground, this parent has engaged his child and simultaneously offered him a realistic challenge.

2 Success! The child stops the ball and kicks it back, as asked. The youngster is clearly enjoying the session and the parent now has his attention and a platform upon which to build.

BALL-FAMILIARITY DRILLS

It is important to develop ball skills from an early age, but this does not mean that children should strive to perfect the Cruyff turn by the time they are three years old. Simple games, like throwing and catching a lightweight ball, help teach children how a ball reacts according to various factors, and will provide valuable foundations upon which to build.

BOUNCING BALL →

The ability to position your body to receive a moving ball requires balance, coordination and agility. During a match, players are often faced with controlling a football that is bouncing on an uneven surface as it moves toward them at high speed. To get into position and control such a ball, he or she will have to make a judgement or prediction about where the ball is going to end up and move accordingly. Senior players will call upon their experiences of similar situations to make such judgements, and bouncing a ball by hand in a confined area is the first step on the way to building up such a body of knowledge.

DRILL DETAIL

- Mark a boundary 20m x 20m (22yds x 22yds) using cones or other markers.
- Introduce children to the area and ask them to bounce a ball on the ground using their hands.
- Remind children that they need to look at the ball, stand lightly on their feet and stay close to the ball.
- This exercise should be practised regularly, though its duration should never exceed ten minutes.

PROGRESSION

- Walking in a large area.
- Reducing the size of the square.
- Increasing the number of children.
- Encouraging the children to move more quickly.

1 A young child bounces a ball on his own within a confined area to improve his coordination.

2 This exercise is a progression of the bouncing-ball drill and teaches players to move their body as they receive the ball. The three white-shirted players and the coach try to throw the ball to one another, while the player in the middle attempts to intercept it. The ball is moved between players using a bounce-pass.

1 Young children should start by dribbling the ball about within their own small, coned-off area. This helps them learn the importance of keeping the ball within a confined area.

BOUNDARIES

Most drills and practice exercises work best when the area being used is defined by a set of boundary cones or markers. From an early age, children must get used to playing sport within prescribed areas. Soccer practice should attempt to replicate the constraints of the game wherever possible, in this case by using rudimentary 'touchlines'.

2 Four players dribble their balls around a set area, carefully avoiding one another. This drill is intended to help children start to learn the skills needed to manoeuvre a ball through a crowded soccer pitch.

WALKING THE BALL ↑

Aspiring soccer players must, of course, learn to move the ball with their feet and this exercise provides an excellent starting point. Just as in the bouncing-ball drill described opposite, a square is marked out by cones, but this time the children move around with the ball at their feet.

DRILL DETAIL

- Mark a boundary 20m x 20m (22yds x 22yds) using cones or other markers.
- Start with one child in the area.
- The child must walk the ball around the area, pushing it forwards using the side of his or her foot.
- This exercise should be practised regularly, though its duration should never exceed ten minutes.

PROGRESSION

- Walking with one child in the area.
- Still walking, but introduce more children into the area.
- Encouraging the children to speed up.
- Reducing the size of the square.

CONE DRILLS

Set up about six or seven cones in a straight line and place a gate made up of two cones at each end. Next, you must demonstrate the exercise yourself. Run through the cones at a steady jog, being careful not to cross your feet over while avoiding going too wide or taking a short-cut over the top of the cones.

Once you have demonstrated the exercise, let the children run through. Invariably, they will run wide and cross over their legs as they go. Demonstrate the exercise again, pointing out how they were doing it, i.e. running wide. Before you let them run through the drill again, put a boundary of cones on each side to help them remain focussed on staying close to the obstacles. You may also find that some children step over the cones; taller cones can help alleviate this problem, but if you don't have any, you will have to rely on gentle reminders.

BALANCE AND COORDINATION

Running in a straight line is all very well, but it is not something footballers are allowed to do very often. On most occasions, players are forced to twist and turn as they try to avoid opponents who block their path forward. For this reason, it is essential that young players work on their balance and coordination so that they can shift their weight from side to side and zig-zag around defenders. And there is no better way to work on lateral movement than the tried-and-trusted method of running around cones.

1

2

3

← RUNNING TOO WIDE

Many children will run in a wide arc around each cone, so to get them closer to the obstacles add in a boundary of cones down each side.

1 The girl in this photograph is running too wide around the cones.

2 The coach stops the session and installs a boundary of discs on each side.

3 With the boundary discs in place, the next child sticks closer to the obstacles.

PROGRESSION
- Jogging on tiptoes.
- Running.
- Double steps.

COMMON FAULTS
- Feet crossing over.
- Stepping over cones. →
- Running in a wide arc around each cone.

DRILL DETAIL
Maximum number of players: Ten.
Equipment: Five or six cones, the taller the better.

As this girl reaches the final cone, the coach throws a ball to her, thereby encouraging her to look up.

A player who is fast and agile, and who can twist and turn before accelerating away from trouble, has an irrefutable advantage over a pedestrian and ponderous opponent. However, coaches and parents often underestimate the importance of teaching children to move efficiently.

MOVEMENT FOR SOCCER

1

2

← AN EFFICIENT RUNNING STYLE

Children should be encouraged to run efficiently from an early age.

1 By running with knees high and their weight on the balls of their feet, players maximize their power and are still able to change direction with ease.

2 The arms are important, too, and should move purposefully in a straight line from pockets to ears.

CANE DRILL ↓

This drill will help to increase coordination and promote a controlled running style. Canes should be spaced at intervals of 18ins (45cm), although this measurement can be varied according to age and shoe size.

Young children should start by simply walking on tiptoes through the canes without touching them. A progression through jogging to running should be achievable within one or two short sessions (no more than ten minutes in duration). The exercise can be repeated with double steps (where the player puts both feet between each gap in the canes before moving on) and skipping. The goal is to have players running, in the manner outlined on the previous page (with high knees and arms moving from pockets to ears), through the cones without having to look down at every step.

USING GATES ↑

A worthwhile training exercise can be quickly reduced to chaos if children who have had their turn get in the way of those moving through the apparatus. A gate, which comprises of two cones or discs, positioned to the side of the active area, will help avoid this situation. Once children have moved through the drill, they run through the gate and return to the starting point.

DRILL DETAIL

Maximum number of players: Ten.
Equipment: Canes or specially designed 'fast-feet ladders', and two cones for a gate.

PROGRESSION

- Walking on tiptoes.
- Jogging.
- Running.
- Double steps.
- Hopping.
- Sideways with double steps.

Once children are running in a controlled fashion and can cope with the lateral movement required to weave in and out of cones, you can begin to work on their speed and, in particular, their acceleration. However, you must be careful not to undo the good work that has gone before by promoting speed at the cost of control.

SPEED AND ACCELERATION

TIPS

- Never presume that children know their left from their right. Wherever possible use colour coding to clarify directions.
- Children should always warm up properly before any exercise that requires them to make sudden changes of direction or speed.

1. STRAIGHT-LINE ACCELERATION ↓

This exercise can be performed equally well with either hoops or canes. If using hoops, you must use an even number to ensure both feet get an equal work-out.

1 The child runs through the obstacles, taking care to put one foot in each hoop.

2 As the player approaches the final hoop, the coach sets a ball 10m (11yds) in front of him.

3 The child completes the obstacles and accelerates toward the ball, which can either be dribbled through a gate or kicked at a target.

DRILL DETAIL
Maximum number of players: Ten.
Equipment: Six or eight hoops.

PROGRESSION
• Jogging.
• Running.

2. TURN WITH ACCELERATION ↓

This drill adds a little soccer realism to the previous exercise. During a match, players will be expected to change direction sharply as they react to loose passes, deflections and interceptions. The first part of this exercise is simply a repetition of the cone drill from page 16. However, when players reach the final hoop, the coach calls out a colour, which should correspond to one of two markers positioned to the extreme left or right of the line of hoops. The player must turn sharply and run toward the appropriate coloured marker.

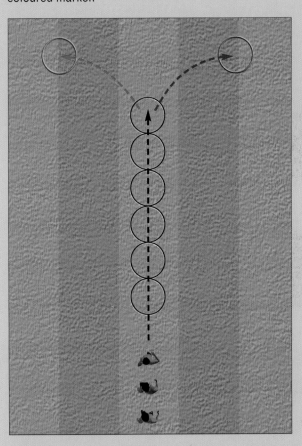

DRILL DETAIL
Maximum number of players: Ten.
Equipment: Six or eight hoops.

PROGRESSION
• Running without a ball.
• Running with a ball.
• Increasing the number of colour-coded points, i.e. not just left and right.

EQUIPMENT

Soccer's enduring appeal and international popularity owes much to the fact that it is a sport that makes no discrimination on economic grounds. Expensive equipment, fancy clothing and vast areas of land are not needed to enjoy the game. A ball, some rudimentary goalposts and a few willing souls are all that's required to partake in the world's best-loved game.

BARGAIN BUYS

To play organized soccer, children, or rather their parents, will need to invest in two items of equipment (three if they decide to play in goal), but even these need not be expensive. There are always bargains available to the discerning shopper, providing they have no objection to wearing footwear endorsed by a fallen idol or shinpads in last season's colourway.

SIZE OF BALL

Many teachers and coaches fail to appreciate that there is no benefit in young children trying, and usually failing, to kick a heavy size-5 football. A size-1 skills ball is ideal for many training drills, while a size-3 is adequate for games involving children between the ages of seven and eleven.

FASHION AND FOOTWEAR

Footwear is the most important item of equipment for a soccer player, and although they do not have to cost a fortune, they can. In recent years, the line between fashion and sportswear has become increasingly blurred and, unsurprisingly, children are now extremely label-conscious when it comes to their soccer boots.

Logically, we know that it really doesn't matter whether an eleven-year-old wears bargain footwear or a pair of the latest Zinedine Zidane-endorsed, brightly coloured offerings from a big-name manufacturer. However, logic does not always speak with a loud voice, and other factors must be considered too.

Confidence can be a fragile thing, and while some children will not care about the number of stripes on their boots, others are undoubtedly affected by the brand they wear and the status they derive from their footwear. Ultimately, parents must decide what type of boots to buy for their child, based on what they can afford, what they feel is appropriate and, finally, what their child wants.

WELL-FITTING BOOTS

Irrespective of brand, if soccer boots are uncomfortable or ill-fitting the child will not strike the ball properly and running will soon become painful. However, this does not mean that every youngster should spend a fortune on the latest kangaroo-skin boots. Even relatively inexpensive footwear can be extremely comfortable, providing you choose well and look after your purchase.

When buying a pair of boots, it is essential that children take their time. Encourage them to try on as many different brands as they can – even those they are initially not keen on. Eventually they will find a pair that fits, both in terms of width and length. It is also important to consider what type of pitches they will be playing on, as this will determine what type of sole they should opt for. Soccer boots come in four main types:

↑ MOULDED

The sole and studs on moulded boots are made from one piece of rubber. The studs are usually fairly short and closely spaced. Moulded boots are best for hard pitches, although those with longer studs are fine on softer ground too.

↑ SCREW-IN STUDS

Traditionally, screw-in boots have just six studs, with each stud screwing directly into the sole of the boot. The great advantage of this system is that studs can be changed to suit the conditions (i.e. long, metal studs for soft pitches and short, rubber studs for firm ground).

↑ ASTRO-TURF

The arrival of the first astro-turf pitches in the 1970s saw the invention of a special type of boot, specifically for this surface. Astro pitches are no longer used at the top level of the game, but the boots are still made to meet the demands of amateur footballers and juniors.

↑ CLEATS/BLADES

A recent innovation on the part of sportswear firms is the cleat-sole boot. These boots are based on designs used in American sports (most notably baseball). They have a one-piece sole unit that is made up of a series of blades or cleats.

← SHINPADS

Football is one of only a few contact sports that are played without padding and body armour. A footballer's only real protection from injury is a pair of shinpads. The laws of the game now include shinguards as part of the compulsory equipment for a player. Any player who does not wear shinguards during a match can be asked to leave the field. But it is not just against the rules to play without pads; it is also against common sense.

← GOALKEEPER'S GLOVES

The junior goalie looking for a pair of gloves will find a bewildering array of designs, each claiming some spurious scientific advantage over the others. The best thing, however, is to opt for a pair that feels comfortable and that offers enough padding to help absorb the impact of a shot.

FREE KICKS

The free kick is the most widely used sanction in Association Football, so it is worth getting to know the rules that apply to its use. Free kicks can be either direct or indirect – and it is essential for all coaches to properly understand the distinction.

ESSENTIAL RULES — FREE KICKS

Soccer is generally an uncomplicated sport, but for young players many of the rules seem obscure and confusing. Parents and coaches must have a clear grasp of the key laws in order to explain them. It is a good idea to summarise the rules, picking out the salient points so that you can communicate them to your players when the opportunity arises during a coaching session or match.

A dangerous tackle will result in the award of a direct free kick.

← DIRECT FREE KICKS

Direct free kicks, as the name suggests, are kicks from which the taker may score without the ball having to touch anybody else first. Direct free kicks must be taken from the place where the incident occurred, except in the event of offences committed by a defending team in their own penalty area, in which case a penalty is awarded rather than a free kick. There are nine main offences that bring about the award of a direct free kick:

1. A kick, or attempted kick, on an opponent.
2. Tripping an opponent.
3. Jumping at an opponent.
4. Charging an opponent in a manner considered by the referee to be either violent or dangerous.
5. Charging or tackling an opponent from behind.
6. Striking, attempting to strike or spitting at an opponent.
7. Holding an opponent.
8. Pushing an opponent.
9. Handling the ball (this, of course, does not apply to the goalkeeper within his own penalty area).

INDIRECT FREE KICKS

A goal can only be scored from an indirect free kick if the ball is touched by more than one player (from either side) on its route to goal. This means that the taker cannot shoot for goal 'direct' from the free kick. The referee will indicate the award of an indirect free kick by raising his arm above his head. He will keep his arm in this position until the ball is touched by a second player. There are currently ten offences that lead to an indirect free kick:

1. Any play that the referee considers to be dangerous (e.g. attempting to kick the ball out of the keeper's hands).
2. Charging fairly (i.e. using the shoulder) but when the ball is not within playing distance.
3. Intentionally obstructing an opponent when not playing the ball.
4. Charging the goalkeeper.
5. When a goalkeeper picks up a ball that has been passed back to him by a team-mate, except where the pass was headed or chested back.
6. Time-wasting, including goalkeepers who hold onto the ball for more than five seconds.
7. A player caught in an offside position when the ball was played forward.
8. Dissent toward the referee.
9. Ungentlemanly conduct.
10. A player takes a corner, throw-in or free kick and touches the ball for a second time before any other player touches it.

A player is allowed to use his arms to hold off an opponent, but only if the ball is within playing distance and the challenge is not deemed dangerous.

KEY FACTS

- The ball must be stationary when the free kick is taken.
- Free kicks awarded to a defending team within its own penalty area can be taken from any other point in the penalty area.
- All opponents must be 10yds (9.15m) from the ball when a free kick is taken.
- The referee will raise his arm to indicate an indirect free kick.
- A goal can only be scored from an indirect free kick if a second player (from either team) touches the ball after the kick has been taken.

ESSENTIAL RULES – BALL OUT OF PLAY

While the ball is in play, the game is uncomplicated. However, as soon as the ball leaves the playing area or the game is forced to stop, things become a little less straightforward ... and invariably junior players will look to their coach for guidance. There are a variety of ways in which a game can be restarted following a break in play. The method employed will vary according to the reason that play was stopped.

KICK-OFF

According to the laws of the game, a match is started by 'a player taking a place kick ... into his opponents' half of the field of play'. This event, which is usually referred to as the 'kick-off', also takes place after half-time and after a goal is scored. All players must be in their respective halves of the field – with the defending team remaining 10yds (9.1m) from the centre-spot – until the ball is played forward.

KEY FACTS: KICK-OFF

- The ball must be played forward from the centre-spot.
- Everybody must be in their respective halves of the field prior to kick-off.
- Players from the defending team are not allowed to enter the centre circle until the ball has been played.

DROP BALL↓

After a temporary break in play, for example when a player is injured as a result of an accident rather than any foul play, the referee will restart the game with what is known as a 'drop ball'. One player from each team is chosen to contest the ball, which is dropped at the place where it was when play was suspended. Neither player is allowed to touch the ball until it has hit the ground, at which point it is deemed in play.

KEY FACTS: DROP BALL

- The ball must bounce before either player strikes it.
- A drop ball is not an opportunity to swing wildly at the ball; the referee can award a free kick if he or she deems that a player's attempt to play the ball constitutes a foul.

GOAL KICK

A goal kick is given when the whole of the ball, having last been touched by a member of the attacking team, crosses the goal-line (excluding the area between the goalposts). Goal kicks are taken from any point on the six-yard box and must be kicked into play beyond the 18-yard box. All opposition players must leave the penalty area until the ball has itself left the area. Any player can take a goal kick, not only the goalkeeper.

CORNER KICK

A corner is awarded when the whole of the ball, having last been touched by a member of the defending team, crosses the goal-line (excluding the area between the goalposts). When taking a corner, the whole of the ball must sit within the quarter-circle at the nearest corner flag. Players from the defending team cannot approach within 10yds (9.1m) of the ball until it is in play (i.e. until it has moved the distance of its own circumference). A goal can be scored direct from a corner.

THROW-IN →

When the whole of the ball crosses the touchline, a throw-in is awarded to the team opposed to the player who last touched the ball. The thrower must have both feet on the ground and be standing on the touchline, or on the ground outside the touchline, as he delivers the ball. He must hold the ball in both hands and deliver it from behind and over his head. If the throw-in is deemed to be illegal or foul, the opposing team will be awarded a throw-in from the same position.

KEY FACTS: THROW-IN

- Both the throw-in taker's feet must be behind the touchline.
- Both feet must be in contact with the floor.
- The ball must travel from behind the taker's head in one continuous movement.

KEY FACTS: GOAL KICK

- The whole ball must cross the dead-ball line for a goal kick to be awarded.
- After a goal kick is taken, the ball must leave the penalty area before a second player (from either team) can touch it.
- Kicks can be taken by any player from any point on the six-yard line.

KEY FACTS: CORNER KICK

- You cannot be offside straight from a corner (this is because the ball cannot travel forwards, without going out of play).
- You can score direct from a corner.

The top two pictures show a 'legal' throw-in technique. The ball is brought forward from behind the player's head while both feet remain on the ground and behind the line. The bottom two pictures, however, show two common faults – foot up and foot over the line.

A SIMPLE RULE

The aim of the offside rule is simple: in short, it is intended to stop forwards from hanging around the goal. Without the rule, strikers would just stand in their opponents' penalty area waiting for long balls to be played forward and the game would descend into farce. To avoid this situation, the offside rule requires there to be two defenders (one of whom is usually a goalkeeper) between an attacker and goal at the time when the ball is played forward by a team-mate.

TEACHING CHILDREN ABOUT OFFSIDE

The best way to explain the rule to children is to illustrate how easy the game becomes if goal-hanging is permitted. To do this, set up a small-sided game and position one attacker from each team just in front of goal. Let each team score a few goals, while you encourage them to hit long balls toward their respective goal-hangers. After a few minutes, stop the action and explain to the players what has been happening and how the offside rule would have prevented the goal-hangers from scoring.

Now you can set up a small-sided game with offsides, and this time restrict touches to three from any one player at any time, as this will encourage the passing of the ball. Explain clearly to the children that, when attacking, they cannot get beyond the final defender until their team-mate has released the ball forwards.

There are several key elements and notable exceptions to the offside rule, each of which coaches should understand.

1. Just because you are in an 'offside position' (i.e. in advance of the last defender with only the 'keeper between you and goal), you are not necessarily offside. To be 'offside' you must be involved in active play. This means that if you are running back toward your own goal and away from the action, you are not in breach of the rule.
2. The ball must be played forward for you to be offside, so, if you shoot into an open goal, having received a square pass from a team-mate, the goal will stand.
3. The critical moment is when the ball is actually played forward. It doesn't matter if you are in an offside position when you receive the ball, it is where you were when you started your run that is important.
4. You cannot be offside from a goalkick, corner or throw-in.
5. You cannot be offside if you were in your own half when the ball was played forward.
6. You cannot be offside if an opponent plays the ball to you.

LEVEL IS ONSIDE

The offside rule previously stated that a player who was level with the last defender (not including the goalkeeper) was offside. However, the rule has recently been changed in favour of the attacking team, so now if you are level, you are onside.

Many adult players regard the offside rule as soccer's unfathomable conundrum. But, in truth, once you strip away the jargon, there's no great mystery behind offside. It is, nevertheless, not the most straightforward concept to explain to children. Thankfully, many junior competitions, particularly those involving small-sided games, play to the spirit of the offside rule rather than the letter of the law.

ESSENTIAL RULES — OFFSIDE

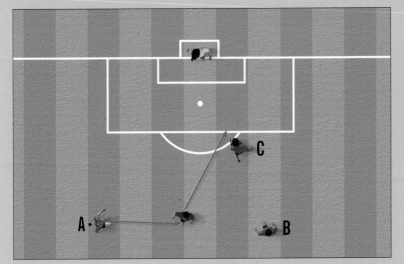

← 1. ONSIDE!

The red team are attacking, and Player A attempts to play a square pass to Player B. However, the pass is cut out by the blue defender who deflects the ball forward into the path of Player C. Although Player C is in an offside position he is deemed to be onside because the ball has not been played forward to him by a team-mate.

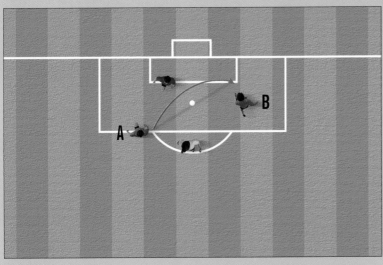

← 2. OFFSIDE!

The blue team are under extreme pressure – their goalkeeper has been beaten by Player A and is left stranded out of his goal. Player A has the ball but, with one defender left to take on, he elects to pass to Player B. Player A had assumed that, with a defender still between his team-mate and goal, Player B was in an onside position. However, with the goalkeeper out of the game, there is only one opponent between Player B and goal. The ball is played forward and the result is a linesman's flag for offside against the red team.

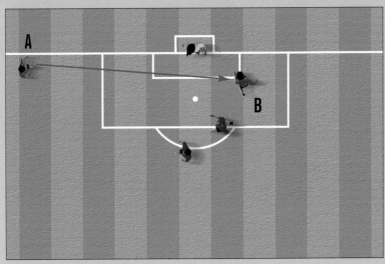

← 3. ONSIDE!

Player A has run down the left wing and, in anticipation, Player B moves ahead of the blue team's defence in the penalty area. Player A crosses the ball to his team-mate who appears to be in an offside position. However, because the ball has not travelled forward, Player B is deemed to be onside.

WARMING UP

2

According to popular wisdom, junior players do not need to warm up because they are 'naturally supple' already. Thankfully, this archaic and potentially dangerous view has been challenged by a new breed of progressive coaches, and today most youngsters expect to go through a warm-up routine before a training session or game.

WARM-UP

It is true that children's muscles are typically more supple than an adult's, but they are not immune from strains and pulls. If players overstretch or twist awkwardly when their muscles are cold, they can sustain a painful and debilitating injury.

Whether warming up before a game or a training session, children should take the time to stretch properly and ensure they are supple enough to perform at their peak. It is also essential that they warm down after exercise.

Throughout the professional game warming up is taken very seriously, but even at junior level, there is no reason why players should not go through a short but thorough warm-up and stretching routine.

If players prepare properly, they will give themselves a better chance of performing to the best of their ability for the duration of a game. Warming up for a training session or match should involve stretching and jogging for 10–15 minutes, depending on the age of the children. Older children will have more patience. Running will get the body temperature and the heart rate up, while stretching will warm the muscles.

← JOG FIRST

Before players begin any stretching, it is advisable to jog gently around the pitch or training field for a few minutes to raise the body temperature and heart rate.

DYNAMIC FLEX VERSUS STATIC STRETCH

There are two ways to stretch. The conventional way is the static stretch, where you stand still and ease into each movement. The second method, called dynamic flex, is where the player moves around as he or she stretches. The experts are currently divided on the relative merits of each approach. Whichever one you choose, the important thing is to ensure that players always stretch in a controlled and unhurried fashion.

GROIN STRETCH ↑

Soccer players are more susceptible to groin strains than most sportsmen. The groin muscles, which are located on the inside of the thigh, can be damaged when a player overstretches, or stretches awkwardly, for a ball or tackle.

1 This is an exaggerated version of a sprinter's starting position. The following muscles are stretched by this exercise: frontal groin area, thigh, calf and Achilles tendon.

2 The player adopts the position shown, applying pressure to his knee to maximize the stretch.

HAMSTRING →

The hamstring (or the rear leg biceps to be more accurate) is located at the back of the leg. It is a muscle group that travels all the way from the lower buttock to the back of the knee. As anyone who has suffered a hamstring tear will tell you (sprinters and speedy wingers are particularly susceptible), this injury is extremely painful. Hamstring injuries always occur suddenly and, while there can be no guaranteed protection, good stretching is the soundest precaution you can take. Stretching hamstrings will also make players more flexible.

1 There are many variations of hamstring stretch, but junior players should not need to get into the elaborate contortions that some professionals indulge in.

2 The leg being stretched is locked straight, while the rear leg supports the body. Both hands are placed upon the leg to apply pressure while the stretch is held for 10–30 seconds.

THIGH STRETCH →

The frontal quad is a very large muscle in the thigh. It is one of the easiest to pull and one of the most difficult to heal. Muscle strains are common, particularly when players are pushing off from a standing start. Good all-round flexibility lessens the chance of strains, and the best way to achieve this is to stretch properly.

1 This popular exercise can be performed assisted, i.e. with a partner, or solo. The key is to move into the stretch gradually.

2 Players should be encouraged to maintain their balance while slowly bringing pressure to bear on the thigh.

THE LOWER LEG: CALF AND ACHILLES STRETCH ↓

The most likely muscle to be affected by cramp is the calf muscle. Most soccer players know the pain of cramp in the calf only too well. The causes of cramp are the subject of much debate. Obstruction of blood/oxygen supply, salt deficiency or deficiency of other body minerals have all been blamed. All no doubt play their part, but muscle fatigue due to prolonged work is clearly a major culprit. Development and preparation of the calf muscle will limit the chances of cramp.

The calf and Achilles tendon are closely linked and often a pain in the Achilles is the result of a blow to the calf muscle. The lower leg is a very sensitive area and, therefore, requires special attention. The Achilles tendon, for example, should not be stretched too quickly or too strenuously.

2

1

1 This exercise stretches the calf and Achilles. It may look awkward, but it is worth practising and getting right. Players' position their weight on the bent, rear leg while the front leg provides extra support. Body weight is positioned centrally.

2 Make sure players avoid the temptation to lean too far forward. This position should be held for 20 seconds before it is repeated using the other leg.

TIPS

- Players must be encouraged to take their time.
  Explain to them that they must ease into each stretch.
- A stable, balanced body position is essential.
  Uneven weight distribution will make exercises more difficult and less effective.
- Players must avoid sharp, sudden movements. Stretching should be smooth and controlled.
- Make sure that players are breathing steadily throughout each exercise.
  Breath should be taken in through the nose and exhaled from the mouth.

BASIC SKILLS

3

Junior players will invariably want to juggle the ball before they can control it, just as they will try to perfect the Cruyff turn before they can hit a sidefoot pass. Such youthful exuberance should not be deterred, but as well as working on their repertoire of attacking skills, children should be encouraged to practise the basics too. It is the fundamental arts of ball control, passing and heading that dominate the average junior soccer match, rather than any more sophisticated skills. A child who has mastered the basics will be an asset to any team.

DIRECTING THE BALL

As players get more confident, they should begin to think about not only stopping the ball but also directing it into a desired position. For example, when controlling a ball in readiness to shoot, players should try to push the ball far enough in front of them so that they can take a stride forward before unleashing their shot. Similarly, when taking a pass on the run, players will need to knock the ball away from any nearby defenders so that they can continue moving forwards. Players should be encouraged to evaluate each situation on its merits and thereby determine how much weight to put behind their first touch.

AVOID THE OLD TRAP

In the past, soccer coaches talked about 'trapping the ball'. However, the technique of stopping a moving ball by placing your foot on top of it is seen today as both risky and ineffective. A far better way for a footballer to bring a ball under control is to cushion it, and the beauty of this approach is that the fundamental technique remains the same whether using foot, thigh, chest or head.

CUSHIONING THE BALL

The aim is to absorb any pace on the ball by meeting it with a cushioned touch. The ball should be given as large an area as possible to land upon and, where possible, the chest, head, thigh or foot should be withdrawn as contact is made. By doing this, the ball is slowed down sufficiently to fall at the feet of the player.

1 **2**

← SIDEFOOT CONTROL – INSIDE OF THE FOOT

The easiest way to control the ball is by using the inside of the foot.

1 The player must stand in a relaxed fashion, with his or her eyes firmly on the ball. As it approaches, the player may need to adjust position to remain in the line of flight. The non-kicking foot is positioned slightly ahead of the other foot, which meets the ball and is then immediately withdrawn at the moment of impact.

2 It is this action of bringing the foot back that cushions the ball into the player's stride. Controlling the ball with the inside of the foot will generally push the ball away from the player's body.

1

2

3

SIDEFOOT CONTROL — OUSTIDE OF THE FOOT ↑

The technique used to control the ball with the outside of the foot is similar to that outlined for the inside of the foot (see opposite). However, greater precision is required as the player has a smaller area of the foot to aim at.

1 The player must turn his leg to offer the ball as flat and large an area as possible to land against.

2 Just as before, the foot is brought back sharply at the moment of impact.

3 This technique is best used to bring the ball in toward the body.

CHECKLIST

CUSHIONING THE BALL

Players must:

1. Stand 'lightly' as the ball approaches.
2. Position themselves in the ball's line of travel.
3. Assess their options and decide which area of the foot or body they will use to control the ball.
4. Look directly at the ball.
5. Position their non-kicking foot ahead of the ball.
6. Use arms for balance.
7. Bring the striking foot back at the moment of impact.

SIMPLE PRACTICE ROUTINE

The easiest way to practise cushioning the ball in a training-session scenario, is for a coach or team-mate to serve the ball from the hands in to a player. The flight of the ball can be varied to make sure that each player is comfortable controlling the ball with foot, chest and thigh. In addition, by varying the pace of the throw, players will have to adjust their body position accordingly, taking a step foward if the ball is served in slowly and stepping back when it comes faster.

↑ CHEST AND THIGH CONTROL

1 The techniques for controlling the ball with chest and thigh are similar. The key to both skills is watching the ball and adjusting your body position to meet it with the appropriate area of the body. Players will also need to show good balance and body strength when using these techniques in a game situation.

2 When using the chest, players should stand on the balls of their feet. The player must get in position early and, at the moment of impact, he must lean back slightly to cushion the ball into the desired position. Thigh control requires an identical set-up, and players must position the thigh at an angle of 45 degrees to the ground. Once contact is made, the leg is lowered slightly to cushion the ball.

3 As the ball drops down, the player must look to regain his or her balance. Quick reactions are vital now, as opponents will look to profit from any hesitancy and sneak in as the ball drops to the ground. The player should endeavour to take a second touch as quickly as possible.

WATCH-THE-BALL DRILL

Whichever technique is used to control the ball, one common requirement is that players must keep their eye on the ball throughout. For youngsters, who are invariably preoccupied with the opponent closing in, or with the top corner of the goal that they are about to score in, looking at the ball is not always that appealing. It is the job of the coach to make sure that keeping an eye on the ball becomes a habit for junior players, and this simple drill will help.

- Three players or more stand in a 10m x 10m (11yds x 11yds) square, which is marked with cones or discs.
- The players stand at equal distances in a circle (or triangle if there are only three) and throw the ball, using chest passes, between themselves.
- They should be encouraged to disguise their passes, as this will help promote concentration and ensure that they remain focussed on the ball throughout.

TOP OF THE FOOT ↑

Cushioning the ball with the top of the foot is a difficult skill to perfect and only the most able players will feel sufficiently confident to attempt it during a match.

1 The top-of-the-foot cushion employs a small area of the boot, and the potential for miscontrolling is great.

2 A steady head is required, while eyes must remain focussed on the ball.

3 At the moment of impact the foot is brought towards the ground, pulling the ball out of the air and to a halt ahead of the player.

STRIKING THE BALL CORRECTLY

As any parent knows, children instinctively strike the ball with the toe of their boot or shoe. The 'toe punt', however, is an inaccurate, unreliable and often painful way of kicking a ball. Any junior player wishing to progress beyond a friendly kickaround in the park must quickly learn to strike the ball properly, using a variety of techniques and kicking areas. Children must feel comfortable in possession of the ball and confident that they can deliver a pass accurately to a team-mate.

KICKING AREAS OF THE FOOT

THE TOP OF THE FOOT
The most powerful contact area of the boot. The sweet spot, as some coaches call it, is used for driving the ball long distances, shooting and clearing.

OUTSIDE OF THE FOOT
Used for bending the ball around opponents. High margin of error compared with the inside of the foot, so usually used only in attacking situations.

THE INSIDE OF THE FOOT
This is the safest area of the foot to use for passing. The wide area on the side of the foot offers improved control and reduces the chances of a poor contact being made with the ball. Whenever possible this is the area of the foot that should be used for passing.

THE INSTEP
Frequently used for passing, crossing, chipping and shooting. The instep offers a good combination of power and accuracy.

← SIDEFOOT PASS

The sidefoot pass – or push pass as it is also known – is best used for passing over short distances along the ground. The technique is simple, although it should still be practised until it becomes second nature.

1 The non-kicking foot is placed alongside the ball.

2 The kicking foot is turned out at right angles to the direction of the pass.

3 The ball is played with the side of the boot, using a firm ankle.

4 Players should aim to strike the middle of the ball to keep the pass on the ground.

5 A full and steady follow-through should be employed.

THE DRIVE ↓

Junior players are usually desperate to kick the ball hard and long. Yet they often fail to appreciate that a powerful strike is the result of good technique rather than brute force. Players should be encouraged to take their time as they approach the ball. A smooth swing and a clean contact with a full follow-through should generate sufficient power without compromising control.

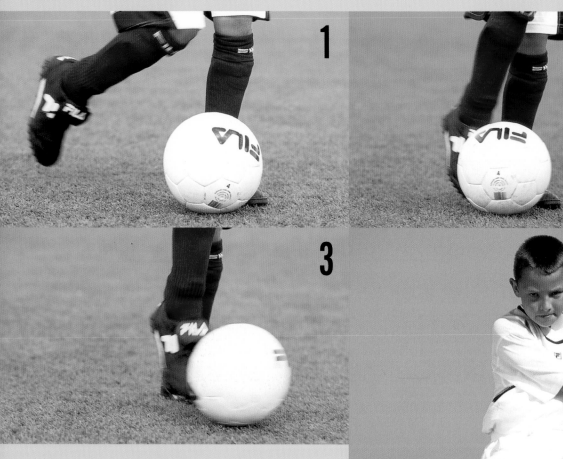

1

2

3

4

1 As the player approaches, he positions his standing foot alongside the ball. His head must remain steady and eyes focussed on the ball.

2 The toes of the striking foot point down toward the ground.

3 The player strikes right across the middle of the ball using the laces or instep.

4 A full follow-through maximizes power and can also aid direction.

THE CHIP ↓

The chip is one of the most difficult techniques to master. It requires not only subtlety of touch but also supreme confidence. Before a player attempts to chip an opponent during a match, he or she should have practised sufficiently to be confident of clearing the person in their way. If a player misjudges a chip or underhits the pass due to a lack of confidence, the results can be embarrassing and costly.

1 Position the non-kicking foot adjacent to the ball.

2 Slide the striking foot underneath the ball, stabbing at it with a sharp motion that propels it up and away.

3 Keep both eyes firmly fixed on the ball.

4 A short follow-through should be sufficient to send the ball in the desired direction.

THE VOLLEY →

The volley is usually used as a shot or a clearance, as in most other circumstances a player will opt to control the ball before playing it. However, in some situations, for example, in the attacking third of the field or when counter-attacking, a volleyed pass may be successfully employed.

KEY TO A SUCCESSFUL VOLLEYED PASS

- It is vital to watch the ball as it descends, adjusting body position to compensate for any change.
- Position the non-kicking foot behind the expected point of impact.
- Aim to strike the bottom half of the ball in the middle, although be careful not to strike the ball underneath, as this would send it straight up into the sky.
- Point the foot and extend the ankle at impact.

CHECKLIST

KICKING A BALL

- Encourage children to use the sidefoot pass when possible.
- Practice sessions should work on both feet.
- The non-kicking foot should be set alongside the ball.
- Players should try to check where they are aiming the ball before striking, but they must also remember to keep their eyes on the ball when they make contact.

VARIETY AND PROGRESSION

When putting on a passing and control session, the most difficult thing for a coach is to retain children's interest. Sidefoot passing does not sound terribly exciting to a junior player, who will invariably have both eyes fixed on the goals and fingers crossed that today is the day for shooting practice.

To gain children's attention, you must make sure that training exercises are varied – even if this means changing a few superficial details while maintaining the central theme of the drill. Concentration will, however, only survive if the session offers achievable challenges and regular progression. For example, a group of six-year-olds will probably struggle to sustain an opposed, one-touch keep-ball session that requires them to use only their weaker foot. However, it may be an ideal practice drill for an older group of children who have already been working on keep-ball sessions for several weeks and who have shown that they can cope with one-touch keep-ball with their stronger foot.

Finally, to ensure successful practice sessions, the coach should work on passing and control often, but never prolonging a single drill for more than about ten minutes.

DRILLS FOR PASSING AND CONTROL

The simple skills of sidefoot passing and cushioned control are all too often neglected on the training ground, as many junior coaches frequently ignore these fundamental techniques in favour of the more glamorous aspects of the game. However, time spent on shooting drills or step-overs rarely brings forth the kind of increased confidence and improved performances that can be achieved by regularly practising the vital arts of passing and control.

HITTING THE WALL

Passing and control can also be practised by players working at home on their own, all it takes is a wall, a ball and a few minutes. Kicking a ball against a wall at different heights, angles and speeds, and then controlling it as it bounces off, can do wonders for a player's control. It is an old technique, but it is nonetheless effective.

← KEEP-BALL SESSIONS

Five players in a circle, passing a football between themselves, in no particular order, constitutes keep-ball in its most basic form. It is, however, an exercise that can be progressed in many ways to test particular strengths and weaknesses. Firstly, the coach can decide upon the number of touches each player can have – three (control, set and pass) is the maximum. Secondly, the coach can decide which foot to use and, finally, he or she can set the session as 'opposed' (i.e. with defenders) or 'unopposed'. An opposed session recreates some of the pressure of controlling the ball in a match situation. The player must get behind the ball early and decide where to pass it before it has arrived.

DRILL DETAIL

1. Space a group of players equidistantly around a circle that is about 20m (22yds) in diameter.
2. Set a boundary of cones around the outside of the circle to prevent the players from extending the circle to make the exercise easier.
3. Get the children to pass between themselves, allowing them three touches each to start with.
4. Work through the progression.
5. This exercise should be practised regularly, though its duration should never exceed ten minutes.

PROGRESSION

1. Unopposed, three touch.
2. Unopposed, two touch.
3. Unopposed, one touch.
4. Opposed, two touch.
5. Opposed, one touch.

SIMPLE PASSING DRILLS

To start with, some young players may struggle to contend with the pressure of a keep-ball session. To help them hone their passing technique and first touch, it may be better to begin with a smaller-scale exercise. A two-player drill is ideal for this purpose, and with subtle variations it can also be used to help more experienced players develop their skills.

← STATIC DRILL

This exercise is basically a controlled version of two players passing a ball between themselves. All the coach needs to do is mark out an area with cones and define the aims of the session. The cones will help prevent the exercise declining into chaos as the two players would otherwise get further and further apart. To start with, the players can have as many touches as they like, but a gradual progression should be employed until they are confidently stroking the ball, first time, with either foot. The coach can also direct the players to control with one foot and pass with the other, or to play passes left-footed from left to right or right-footed in the opposite direction.

DRILL DETAIL

1. Mark out a regtangular section of pitch 6m x 1m (6.5yds x 1.1yds) using cones or similar markers.
2. Position players at opposite ends of the marked area.
3. Get players to pass between themselves, allowing them three touches each to start with.
4. Work through the progression.
5. This exercise should be practised regularly, though its duration should never exceed ten minutes.

PROGRESSION

1. Three touch, either foot.
2. Two touch, either foot.
3. One touch, either foot.
4. Two touch, stronger foot.
5. One touch, stronger foot.
6. Two touch, weaker foot.
7. One touch, weaker foot.

10m

2m

P2

P2

P3

P1

P1

| ← - - - | run |
| ← — | pass |

↑ PASSING ON THE MOVE

Once players have mastered the static drill, they can move onto a more 'game-realistic' drill, which incorporates movement. This time a larger pitch is used – 10m x 2m (11yds x 2.2yds) – and a minimum of three players is required. Players run with the ball to a cone positioned at the centre of the pitch, they then pass the ball to a colleague who is commencing a run in the opposite direction from the baseline. The second player then runs with the ball back to the middle and, in turn, passes the ball to a third player.

DRILL DETAIL

1. Mark out a rectangular section of pitch 10m x 2m (11yds x 2.2yds) using cones or similar markers.
2. Position cones halfway down the length of each side of the pitch.
3. Explain to players how many touches they are allowed and which foot should be used to control and which to pass.

GETTING STARTED ↓

The only problem with ball juggling is that many young players find it very difficult to get started and often become frustrated that they cannot make instant progress. The best way to avoid this is if they start by letting the ball bounce before attempting to kick it up toward their own hands.

1 The ball should be spun as it is dropped, with the player flicking his or her hands up and away from the body to put backspin on the ball to bring it back toward the body.

2 The next step is to try to kick the ball before it has touched the ground. Encourage players to use both feet, even at this early stage.

3 The aim is to get the player juggling in the following sequence: spin from hands, bounce, right foot, bounce, left foot, catch. Once this sequence is being regularly achieved the 'bounces' can be removed and the ball moved from right foot to left foot.

Not so long ago, many coaches frowned upon their players spending time juggling a ball around the training ground. Thankfully, nowadays attitudes have changed, and the benefits of good juggling skills are widely appreciated. The great thing about ball juggling is that young players cannot get enough of it. Children are always desperate to hone their skills, copying tricks from older friends and working on the flick-ups that they have seen on TV. It is also a skill that players can practise on their own, and by doing so they will improve their close control, balance and confidence when dealing with balls that arrive at an awkward height. And did we mention that it is fun too?

JUGGLING

1 Juggling the ball with both feet is not as easy at looks. Players must stand lightly on the balls of their feet, keeping their eyes focussed on the football throughout.

2 Players must control their strike, making a firm but not heavy contact. As the ball rises into the air, the player should adjust his or her body position so that the opposite foot is directly underneath the point at which the ball will come down.

↑ **JUGGLING WITH LEFT AND RIGHT FOOT**

CHECKLIST

JUGGLING
Players must remember to:
• Stay relaxed.
• Avoid planting their weight heavily on their standing foot (otherwise they will not be able to adjust their body position).
• Keep their eyes on the ball.
• Strike the ball firmly with the top of the boot.
• Practise using both feet.

This player is standing too heavily, with his feet flat on the ground. He will not be able to react and reposition his body to meet the ball as it descends.

INDIVIDUAL SKILLS

As a player's skills develop, he or she should try to
control the ball in as many different ways as possible.
This will help that player improvise during games when
the ball arrives awkwardly. The back of the heel is a good
surface to control the ball as is the outside of the foot,
but as with all ball skills, control and accuracy only come
with practice.

THIGH JUGGLE ↑

Juggling is all about innovation, so when a player is
happy keeping the ball up with his or her foot, the next
step is to employ other parts of the body. The thigh is an
obvious choice, as it has a perfect surface for juggling
as it is wide and reasonably flat.

The juggle should begin in the normal way, with a spin
and then the feet, but once the ball is airborne it should
be pushed up to chest height. The thigh is then
positioned at right angles to the body and is brought up
to meet the ball as it arrives at waist height.

FLICK-UPS

Flicking the ball in the air is something that all young players love to attempt. It provides a golden opportunity to show off, and even many professionals use a fancy flick to pick up the ball before taking a throw-in or corner kick rather than use their hands. These skills have no real application or value to competitive football and should be restricted to use on the training ground. Nevertheless, they look good, are great fun and help maintain children's interest.

THE TOE FLICK ↓

1 The player leans forwards slightly and drags the ball back towards his left foot, using the sole of his right boot.

2 The ball rolls up the left boot, which is flicked up sharply as contact is made.

3 The action of flicking up the left foot sends the ball flying into the air.

THE ARDILES FLICK ↓

1 The player leans forwards to his left and drags the ball up the back of his standing leg (in this case the left) using the sole of the other foot.

2 As the ball reaches the calf, the player takes his right foot away from the ball.

3 He brings up his left foot, striking the ball with his heel.

4 The ball flies up and over his head.

HEADING

Most junior players do not like heading the ball, but it remains an essential area of the game and one that they should strive to master. The best way to overcome the fear of heading is through gentle encouragement and regular practice. However, practice sessions should always be kept brief, as it is not recommended that junior players repeatedly head a hard ball for prolonged periods. There are three main types of header, and each is outlined below.

DEFENSIVE HEADER →

Power and height are the aims for a defensive header.

1 To achieve the necessary elevation and power, players must get beneath the flight of the ball as early as possible.

2 Players should aim to head through the bottom half of the ball.

3 A full follow-through will ensure that sufficient force is applied to send the ball safely away from danger.

ATTACKING HEADER →

In direct contrast to the defensive header, attacking players should aim to direct their headers down.

1 An early jump will help achieve the extra height necessary to direct an attacking header.

2 Forwards should strive to get above the ball's flight so that they can head through the top half of the ball.

3 Power and direction are vital, and, if possible, players should aim to send the ball down and towards the corners of the goal.

← CUSHIONED HEADER

Controlling the ball with the head is a difficult skill that requires both coordination and a subtle touch. The technique used to cushion the ball down to the floor or into the path of a team-mate is similar to that employed when controlling the ball with the chest.

1 Players must aim to get beneath the ball as early as possible, manoeuvring into position so that the ball drops on to the head.

2 At the moment of impact, the player pulls his head back slightly to cushion the ball.

3 The ball drops gently to the ground at the player's feet.

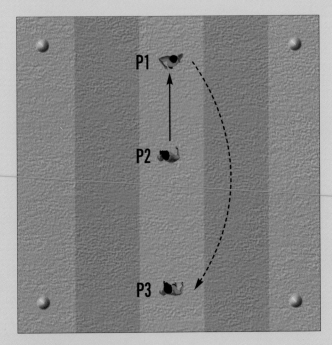

P1

P2

P3

← PRACTICE DRILL

The following practice drill will help build confidence and improve the heading technique of all players.

Player 1 throws the ball to Player 2, who in turn heads the ball back over the server and to Player 3. After each header, the players rotate.

DRILL DETAIL

1. Mark a boundary 10m x 10m (11yds x 11yds) using cones or other markers.
2. Start by serving the ball yourself to ensure an accurate delivery.
3. Remind players of the need for accuracy.
4. This exercise should be practised regularly, though its duration should never exceed ten minutes.

PROGRESSION

1. Heading to a player 10m (11yds) away.
2. Expand the length of the playing area.
3. Add in an extra player just in front of Player 2 to act as a defender.
4. Replace Player 3 with two differently coloured markers in the left- and right-hand corners. As the ball is delivered, the coach calls out the colour of one of the makers (e.g. 'red') and the player must head toward the appropriate corner.

CHECKLIST

HEADING

Remind players that they should:

- Avoid closing their eyes when heading the ball.
- Use their arms for balance – though avoid jumping with elbows high.
- Concentrate on meeting the ball at the highest point possible
- Get into position early and before their opponents.

INDIVIDUAL SKILLS

Junior players need very little motivation when it comes to learning individual skills. All youngsters seem to enjoy learning new tricks and techniques, particularly anything that involves fancy footwork or shooting at goal. However, youthful exuberance can be a destructive force too, and it is the job of the coach or parent to focus children's learning so that their energies are channelled into a structured learning programme that offers a consistent level of progression.

VOLLEYING

A ball in mid-flight, arriving at knee height, is a tempting prospect to the junior player. Instinctively, he thinks 'whack it hard', but invariably such an approach leads to no more than an embarrassing air shot or a hopelessly inaccurate strike. The job of the coach is to encourage players to make control rather than power the priority when volleying.

THE QUEST FOR POWER →

Junior players regard the volley as an opportunity to kick the ball hard. With the ball off the ground already, youngsters feel confident that they can strike it with a clean contact – just as a golfer does when hitting the ball from a tee peg. But all too often, the result is a wild swing, characterized by lots of extraneous body movement and followed by a swift look up to see where the ball has gone.

MAINLY A SHOT, SOMETIMES A CLEARANCE

The volley is occasionally used as a pass (see page 45 for more details), but more usually it is used as a shot when there is neither the time nor the space to control a ball in flight. Defenders may also be forced to volley the ball clear when faced with a similar situation and under pressure from opponents.

1 The key to a successful volley is to keep the head still and the eyes fixed on the ball.

2 A clean contact is more important than a powerful swing. Strike through the ball into a full follow-through.

CHECKLIST

VOLLEY

Players must remember to:
1. Concentrate on control over power.
2. Look at the ball as they strike it.
3. Keep their head still and over the ball when shooting.

VOLLEYING TECHNIQUE ↓

BALL ARRIVING STRAIGHT ON

The head should be kept steady, with the eyes looking down at the ball throughout. The non-kicking foot is positioned behind the ball – further back if the ball is to be played early in its flight. The ankle of the striking foot is extended and the knee raised as the ball approaches. Contact should be made with the instep, striking halfway down the back of the ball. The head remains down as the player completes a full, straight follow-through.

BALL ARRIVING FROM THE SIDE

The non-kicking foot faces the target in a position sideways on to the ball's line of flight. Eyes are fixed firmly on the ball and the head remains steady throughout. As the ball arrives, the leading shoulder drops away and the body rotates around the standing leg, which supports the player's weight. The kicking foot points outwards and is swung across the body, making contact halfway down the back of the ball.

1 A cushioned volley can be used to pass the ball over short distances.

2 The side of the foot is best used for this technique. Players must get into position early and strike the ball with the inside of the foot for maximum control.

3 A short follow-through is all that is required to send the ball to its target.

← VOLLEY PRACTICE

When practising volleying, it is essential that players have a target to aim at, and ideally this should be a goal. Set players at the edge of the penalty area and serve them the ball, alternating deliveries from the penalty spot and from a position to the side. Strikers must aim to hit the ball into the corners of the goal, while defenders must aim to clear the crossbar of the goal.

The art of bending the ball is one that cannot easily be taught and learned within the constraints of a group training session. Once the basic technique has been explained, it is down to the individual player to practise until a breakthrough is achieved. Some players seem to have an almost natural predisposition to curling the ball – approaching from a slight angle and clipping round the ball with the inside of the foot – others, however, struggle to master this technique without hours of practice.

BENDING THE BALL

TO SWERVE OR NOT TO SWERVE

Some footballers use the swerve pass as a matter of course, bending the ball irrespective of whether passing to a team-mate two or twenty yards (two or eighteen metres) away. When correctly judged, a swerving pass can play the ball neatly into the path of a forward-running team-mate. However, it is far simpler to judge the pace and angle of a ball played straight. Junior player should be advised to only bend the ball in attacking situations or when there is no other alternative.

The ability to swerve the ball can be invaluable in the attacking third of the pitch. Passes around defenders, curling free kicks and, best of all, bending shots, can all be extremely effective.

BENDING THE BALL – TECHNIQUE ↓

Whether shooting, crossing or simply passing to a team-mate, the basic technique for bending the ball remains the same. The standing foot is placed to the side of the ball and just behind it. Eyes remain fixed on the ball throughout, while the head points slightly downwards and is kept still. For a right-footed kick, the striking boot comes across the ball from left to right. The inside of the foot makes contact with the ball just to the right of centre, and the right leg continues on its inside–outside path into a full follow-through.

Bending the ball in the opposite direction, i.e. left to right for a right-footed player, uses the outside of the foot, and it is, therefore, a more difficult skill to master. Since a smaller striking area is used, it is difficult to generate both power and direction. This time, contact is made to the left of centre of the ball, and the striking foot moves on a path from outside to inside.

1 To bend the ball from right to left using his right foot, this player approaches the ball with his body open to the target.

2 The non-kicking foot is positioned to the side of the ball and just behind it, and the player leans back slightly to get the necessary elevation on the shot. His eyes remain fixed on the ball throughout.

3 The kicking foot makes contact with the ball just to the right of centre, and the right leg continues on an inside-to-outside path into a full follow-through.

TIPS

- Players must remember to graze across the ball rather than strike right through it.
- It is important that players do not quit on the shot – confidence and a clean contact are required.
- Encourage players to employ a full follow-through.

SHOOTING PRACTICE

SHOOTING DRILLS

Junior players are usually full of enthusiasm and energy when offered the chance to practise their shooting. As a general rule, any exercise that involves goals and footballs will have children captivated. However, to maintain their attention, you must make sure that each drill is well organised.

← USE CONES TO FOCUS ATTENTION

The aim with any shooting exercise should be for players to direct their shots into the corners of the goal. If a shot is placed in any of the four corners, the goalkeeper will struggle to save it. The very best goalscorers develop the ability to ignore the 'keeper, seeing only the spaces around him or her and, invariably, guiding their shots into the four places where a shot-stopper has no chance of making a save. With junior players, the best way to get them focussing on finding the corners of the goal is to set cones on the goal-line just inside the posts. The players can then aim to guide their shots between cones and post.

1 Accuracy is everything when it comes to shooting practice, and the presence of a goalkeeper can often divert players from their main aim of putting the ball in the corner of the goal.

2 On this occasion the player has been asked by his coach to guide the ball into the bottom right corner.

Players can hone their aim and build their confidence by shooting into the corners of an unguarded net. A cone placed in each corner will encourage them to work on their accuracy.

← SHOOTING UNOPPOSED

Whenever possible, strikers should try to send their shots angling across the goalkeeper and in toward the far post. The theory behind this approach is that if the 'keeper gets a hand on the ball, he or she is just as likely to push it back into the path of an onrushing attacker. The drill illustrated on these pages involves players simply running onto either a static ball or a pass from a server (usually the coach) and directing the ball into the far corner of the goal. Players should switch sides after two or three turns, so that by the end of the session each of them has struck a shot from left to right and one from right to left.

DRILL DETAIL
- Coach sets up with a stack of balls just outside the semi-circle on the edge of the penalty area.
- Players can either run with the ball or they can exchange passes with the server before shooting.
- Cones are placed in the goal to define the key target areas.

← PROGRESSION
- Strong foot shooting, hitting a static ball.
- Strong foot shooting, moving ball.
- Weaker foot shooting, hitting a static ball.
- Weaker foot shooting, moving ball.

1 Players stand in a line and take turns to run at the goal. A cone is positioned on the edge of the penalty area, and as each player reaches it the coach calls out left or right. The player must then move to the appropriate side of the cone and shoot for the farthest corner of the goal.

2 In this case, the player has been told to go to the right, and his shot has been directed successfully inside the left-hand post.

SHOOTING PRACTICE

The drill on the previous page will help junior players work on the accuracy of their shooting, but when it comes to a game situation, footballers rarely have the chance to venture into the penalty area unopposed. Defenders will do everything they can to stop an attacker from getting in a shot, and all players should learn to contend with the problems of controlling and striking the ball while under pressure from an opponent.

1 The ball is passed into space by a coach and the two players leave their marks and run toward it.

2 The player in red reaches the ball first as his opponent tries to close him down.

3 The attacker knows he cannot hesitate as the white-shirted defender is closing in, so he shoots for goal.

1 Both players line up shoulder to shoulder and with their backs to goal, 25m (27yds) out. The coach acts as server and stands facing the two players.

2 After a count of three, the coach throws the ball over the two players' heads and in the direction of goal.

3 The players turn and contest the bouncing ball with the aim of winning possession and shooting for goal.

4 The player in white wins the ball and shoots at goal under pressure from his opponent, who inadvertently acts as a defender.

↑ EVERYBODY WANTS TO BE A STRIKER

During a typical training session, you will invariably find that most players want to be centre-forwards, while nobody wants to be a defender. The good thing about the training exercise illustrated on this page, however, is that everybody can play the role of striker. The basic principle is simple: two players compete for a bouncing ball in the penalty area and whoever wins the ball shoots for goal. Both players are told they are strikers, but inadvertently they act as defenders too, putting pressure on the ball and challenging one another as they vie for possession.

DRILL DETAIL
- Set two players 25m (27yds) from goal.
- Tell both players they are 'strikers'.
- After a count of three, throw the ball over the players' heads for them to contest.
- Position cones in the goal as an additional target.
- Remind children that it is a training exercise and that foul play can lead to injuries.

PROGRESSION
- Three players contesting the ball.
- Increase the number of players contesting the ball to a maximum of four.

RUNNING WITH THE BALL

Junior coaches spend much of their time discouraging players from running with the ball, but nobody wants a team of robots who always go for the 'safe' option. Fortunately, young players can never entirely resist the temptation to run with the ball and take on their opponents. As a result, the entertaining sight of an attacker dribbling past a marker remains a common feature of the junior game. However, dribbling is more than just ineffective showmanship, and a flash of individual skill can often be the only way to overcome a packed defence.

←DRIBBLING ESSENTIALS

To beat an opponent with dribbling skills, players must learn the key arts of:

1. Close control – the ball should never be closer to an opponent than to the attacker in possession.
2. Changing direction or pace – to get past an opponent, a swift and unexpected change of pace and direction is required.
3. Disguise – whether using a change of pace, a Cruyff turn or a step-over, players must learn to disguise their true intentions.

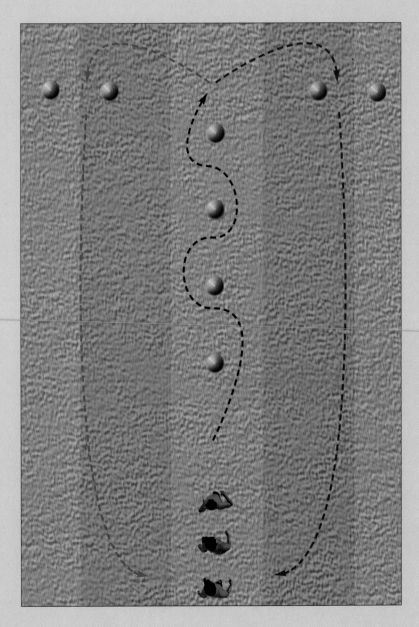

← MIND THE CONES

The best way for junior players to learn the importance of keeping the ball close to their feet is by dribbling through cones. It is an old routine, but it works. Cones are set up in a straight line with a gate at each end, and players must simply dribble their way around each cone. If players begin to run too wide, a line of boundary cones can be put on either side.

Players should be encouraged to look at the ball but also to look up regularly and check the position of the cones. Both feet should be used and players should also practise using both the inside and the outside of the foot.

CHANGING DIRECTION

Experienced wingers and strikers will usually have a host of tricks that they use to jink past defenders. We have chosen two such techniques that can be mastered by the junior player.

← THE MATTHEWS

The simplest way to trick past a defender is to use a dummy, or as it is commonly known 'The Matthews' move. The attacking player, whom we assume to be right-footed, advances toward his opponent and shapes to move to the left. He puts his weight onto his left foot and drops the corresponding shoulder. His right foot begins to move toward the ball as though he is going to strike it across his body; however, at the last moment he switches his weight to the right side and pushes the ball away with the outside of the boot. The defender should be suitably deceived and, having followed the initial movement, will have no chance of readjusting in time to stop the attacker's run.

1 The attacker moves forward and signals his intention to take on the defender who blocks his path forward.

2 By lowering his shoulder and shifting his weight onto his left-hand side, the attacker suggests he is planning to take on the defender down the left.

3 The defender reads the attacker's body movement and begins to move to his right, but he has been deceived and, using the outside of his right boot, the attacker quickly switches direction.

4 The defender has no time to adjust his body position, as the attacker knocks the ball past him on the right and moves into space.

↑ THE STEP-OVER

The step-over works in the same way as The Matthews, and is intended to dupe defenders into committing themselves to moving in the wrong direction. There are two types of step-over that have become popular in the modern game. The first requires the use of just one foot and is a step over the ball from outside to inside, followed by a flick away using the outside of the same foot.

The second type of step-over is for players who are both confident and competent with both feet, as it requires a right-foot approach followed by a left-footed take away (or vice versa).

1 Step-overs require balance, deception and a swift change of direction. You must also be confident that you have both the skill and pace to make the move work.

2 The idea is to make the defender believe that you intend to attack down the right-hand side, but by stepping over and round the ball from inside to out, you give yourself the opportunity to take the ball away with your left foot down the opposite side.

3 As the attacker pushes the ball away with his left foot, the defender is thrown off balance, thus giving the attacker vital seconds in which to get away.

4 The move is a success and the attacker heads off into space while the defender has to turn and go after him.

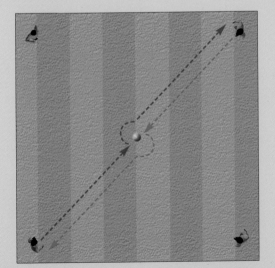

← PRACTISING DUMMIES AND STEP-OVERS

Set up a square 20m x 20m (22yds x 22yds) and place one player with a ball in each corner. Players at opposite corners run toward the middle of the square, which is marked with a cone, but before they reach the centre, they perform a dummy or step-over and switch direction. Players then accelerate to the relevant marker and the next two players repeat. The exercise continues until all players have attempted the move from each corner. Note: this exercise should not be attempted by young players who might fail to make the turn and thereby run into one another.

CRUYFF TURN →

The Cruyff turn, which was named after the famous Dutch player of the 1970s, is a move that most junior players are eager to learn. The player shapes to strike the ball, but instead of making contact with the instep, flicks the ball behind his standing foot using the inside of the boot, and moves it onto the opposite foot. The player should now have space either to make a pass or run with the ball. Players should not overuse the Cruyff turn. The move can become predictable and easy to read if it is used too often. Ideally, players should be able to employ this technique with either foot.

1 Deception is the key to this skill. Players must convince their opponents that they are about to strike the ball.

2 The standing foot should be planted next to the ball and the corresponding arm should be thrown out, mimicking the set-up for a shot or cross.

TURNS

DRAG BACK →

The drag-back turn is used to help players manoeuvre their way out of tight situations. The player can either use the turn to change the angle of attack or, alternatively, to turn through 180 degrees. The latter is particularly useful to strikers trying to turn a marker in the penalty area. In both cases, the technique remains the same. However, this skill should never be used when defending, and players must be careful not to push the ball too close to their marker when luring him into a tackle.

1 The attacker nudges the ball forwards to induce a lunge from his unwitting opponent.

3 The striking foot is checked at the last moment and the ball is flicked behind the player's standing foot.

4 The defender is committed and the attacker now has space in which to manoeuvre.

5 The attacker's successful Cruyff turn has enabled him to pick out a team-mate with a measured cross rather than a hopeful punt.

In tight situations, for example in and around the penalty area, attacking players will often need to make space for themselves so that they can cross the ball or get in a shot. In most cases, they will also need to change direction so that they can direct the ball forward or into a team-mate. However, 'turning' under pressure requires close control, balance and sufficient skill to deceive an opponent.

2 The defender duly obliges, committing himself to a tackle, and the forward places a foot on top of the ball and drags it back.

3 The defender's momentum carries him forward, leaving the attacker to move away from danger.

4 The defender is committed, and the attacker pushes the ball past his stranded marker.

INSIDE AND OUTSIDE HOOKS →

Hooking the ball with the inside or outside of the boot is the most straightforward way to turn a defender. For a right-footed player, the inside hook takes the ball across the body and to the left, while the outside hook moves it away from the body and to the right. The technique for both is the same. The boot curls, or hooks, around the ball and guides it around as the standing leg pivots to push the player forward. When using the inside and outside hooks, an attacker can gain valuable advantage over a marker by dropping his shoulder in the opposite direction of the intended turn.

1 Players must aim to keep the ball close to their foot as they move around. If the ball moves too far away from the foot then the turn will be wide and, in a match situation, defenders would have a better chance of stealing the ball.

2 The player curls his foot around the ball, hooking it with the inside to bring it across his body and using the outside to take it away from his body.

3 The standing leg pivots to push the player in the direction of the ball. This skill requires both balance and fast feet, so it should be practised regularly until players feel confident turning in a relatively confined area.

STOP TURN ↓

The stop turn can be extremely effective but it can also end in embarrassment. It is used to switch directions suddenly, and often when running at full speed. Players should be careful when placing their foot on top of the moving ball... slip-ups are not only embarrassing but also painful. The stop-turn is not recommended in wet or greasy conditions.

1 Without warning, the attacker simply puts a foot on top of the rolling ball to stop it.

2 The element of surprise, means that the defender continues on for longer on the original path, giving the attacker time to turn around and collect the stationary ball.

3 When stepping over the ball, players often get their legs tangled up because they try and turn too sharply.

4 Having successfully completed the stop-turn, the player moves off with the ball under control.

PRACTISING TURNS →

Any turn can be practised in one of two ways. The simplest method is to get players lined up shoulder to shoulder on the six-yard box in readiness for your whistle. When the whistle is blown, players must run toward the edge of the penalty area, when they reach the 18-yard line, they must turn sharply and run back to the six-yard box, where they turn again. The exercise can be repeated until each turn has been practised.

Alternatively, a square 20m x 20m (22yds x 22yds) is marked out and up to ten players are introduced to the square with a ball each. The players dribble around the square until they hear the coaches whistle or shout, at which point they must turn using the required technique. The advantage of this method is that players must avoid bumping into one another, just as they will have to avoid other players when turning in a crowded penalty area.

FINISHING ONE-VERSUS-ONE

There is no more enjoyable training exercise for junior players than a one-versus-one session with the goalkeeper. The 'keeper will enjoy the chance to take on his or her outfield team-mates, while everybody else revels in the opportunity to score goals. From the coaches' point of view it is also a session that consolidates the lessons of earlier training drills, particularly those concerning dribbling and finishing skills.

DRILL ORGANIZATION

To make this drill run smoothly, the coach must ensure that the penalty area never gets clogged up by players. A gate should be used as a queuing point for all players waiting their turn, and once players have completed the drill they should follow a path around the edge of the pitch back to the gate. Balls should be returned from the goal by the goalkeeper if on target, or collected by the striker if they miss. Players must also wait for the coach to give a signal before taking their turn.

The attacker feigns to shoot and sends the goalkeeper to ground, leaving him free to move the ball onto his left foot and fire into the unguarded half of the goal.

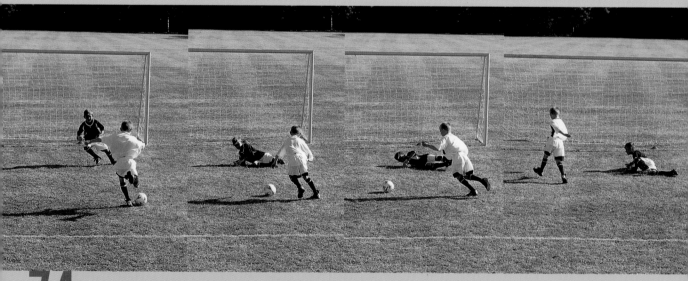

As the goalkeeper comes off his line, the attacker shapes to move left but dummies over the ball and comes back onto his right side. The keeper, however, is already committed and is left on the ground.

TAKING ON THE 'KEEPER

The attacker is set on a mark around 25m (27yds) from goal and must run forward to take on the 'keeper using any skill or trick before shooting for goal. The 'keeper can move forward from the goal-line and close the shooting angle, thereby adding match realism. From an attacking point of view, the aim should be to induce the 'keeper to commit to a challenge, making it simple to go around him or her and shoot into the net.

FREESTYLE OR SPECIFIC SKILL

The coach can set this drill as either freestyle, i.e. the attacking player can use any skill to beat the 'keeper, or alternatively he or she can request that the outfield players use a particular move to go around the 'keeper. If the coach opts for the latter, the specified move should be communicated to the player without the 'keeper hearing, otherwise the goalkeeper will have an unrealistic advantage.

TRICKS USED TO COMMIT A GOALKEEPER

- Feigning to shoot. The player shapes to shoot, but instead of striking the ball, cuts it to the side and around the 'keeper.
- Rolling foot over the ball. The attacker deceives the goalie into anticipating a shot by shaping to strike the ball but rolling a foot over the top of it instead. The 'keeper dives and the striker chips into the unguarded net.
- Step-over. By running the ball right up to the 'keeper, a player can use the step-over move to cut a path to goal. The 'keeper commits to the dummy and goes to ground, leaving the attacker to guide the ball forward to goal.

GOALKEEPING

5

Goalkeepers are so often forgotten when it comes to training, and traditionally they have been left to follow the same routines and drills as their outfield colleagues. However, the position of goalkeeper is a specialist one, which requires tailored practice sessions and individual coaching.

A typical group of junior players will be made up almost exclusively of wannabe centre-forwards. There may be the occasional winger or even a midfielder, but invariably there will be few budding young defenders and fewer still when it comes to aspiring custodians. However, with a little gentle encouragement, some pointed reminders about how important the goalkeeper is and the promise that he or she will have the chance to dive around the penalty area, then volunteers should be forthcoming.

GOALKEEPER TRAINING

← SELECTING A 'KEEPER

When faced with two or more volunteers, however, the coach is called upon to use his or her judgement to decide which player is best suited to the job of goalkeeper. In the past, a player's height was used almost exclusively as the determining factor when picking a 'keeper. However, today coaches should be encouraged to consider more than just size and stature. Height is, of course, still a significant factor, but you should also take into account the following:

- **CONFIDENCE:** Goalkeepers must be bold characters who are willing to throw themselves into the thick of a penalty-area scrum.

- **COMMUNICATION:** As the last line of defence, the goalkeeper can play a vital role in organizing the players in front of them. Goalkeepers must also be willing to shout clearly when leaving their line to claim a cross.

- **HANDLING:** A tall 'keeper who cannot catch will be less effective than a player who is smaller but who has safe hands.

- **AGILITY:** Speed off the line and the ability to jump high to reach a cross are of major importance to the aspiring 'keeper.

- **DISTRIBUTION:** In the modern game, goalkeepers must be confident kickers of the ball – a player who can kick the ball a long way with either foot will be a major asset.

When looking for a goalkeeper, volunteers are not always forthcoming.

← SPECIALIST TRAINING

Once a goalkeeper has been selected, the next job is to make time for a one-on-one coaching session. Ideally, a second coach should be used specifically to train a team's goalkeeper. If, however, that is not possible, the 'keeper should be given specialist training before or after the usual squad session.

While the white-shirted outfield player hones his kicking skills, the goalkeeper gets to practise his catching technique.

HANDLING

With a little judicious coaching, young goalkeepers can make dramatic improvements to their shot handling. The first thing they must learn is how to position their hands when taking a shot. If the ball is above chest height they must employ the 'W' shape; if below the chest, the 'scoops' are used. For both techniques the body positions are largely the same. To practise the Ws and the scoops, the coach can simply throw the ball to the goalkeeper at various heights from a distance of around 10m (11yds).

THE 'W' SHAPE ↓
The Ws are used to deal with shots and crosses played at or above chest height.

1 The hands are placed in front of the body, with fingers spread wide and thumbs touching or close to each other.

2 The player should try to cushion the ball into his hands. His eyes remain fixed on the ball and his head is still throughout.

3 With the ball safely in both hands the 'keeper brings the ball down toward his chest.

CHECKLIST

BODY POSITION — Ws AND SCOOPS
- Head remains still throughout.
- Eyes stay fixed on the ball.
- Player stands lightly on the balls of the feet.
- Feet are shoulder-width apart.
- Hands are at waist height, with palms open.

THE SCOOPS ↓

The scoop technique is used to catch crosses and shots played below chest height.

1 As the ball approaches, the hands are positioned with palms facing out.

2 The ball strikes the goalkeeper's chest, and the hands are closed around it in a cupping motion.

3 The chest is relaxed and the ball is wedged between body, arms and chin.

GROUND SHOTS ↓

The scoop technique is used, albeit in a slightly adapted form, for shots played along the ground.

1 This time the 'keeper moves down to a kneeling position as the ball approaches.

2 The leading foot is positioned side-on to the angle of the shot, while the other leg closes in to offer a secondary obstacle should the ball slip through the 'keeper's fingers.

3 The 'keeper collects the ball and gathers it up, clutching it to his chest.

CROSSES

Learning how to claim a cross effectively is one of the biggest challenges facing an aspiring goalkeeper. It is a skill that requires judgement, safe hands, confidence and strength. Some goalkeepers never master this vital skill, preferring to leave their defenders to contend with any ball outside the six-yard box. Others, by contrast, are too impulsive and charge off their line at the slightest opportunity. Junior players must learn to evaluate each situation, so that they can decide whether to claim a particular cross or stay on their line.

HIGHEST POINT ↓

When claiming a cross, goalkeepers must endeavour to catch the ball at the highest point possible, as by doing so they make it impossible for an outfield player to reach it ahead of them. However, before rushing to reach any cross, goalkeepers must determine whether or not they can actually reach it.

1 Goalkeepers must wait until the cross has been struck. It is dangerous to anticipate what an opponent is going to do. Once the ball has been played, they must assess the trajectory and pace of the cross to decide whether it can be reached ahead of any attackers.

2 Shout! Goalkeepers must let defenders know what they plan to do. Crashing into a team-mate and missing the ball can be both costly and embarrassing. Players should try to take off with one foot to maximize the height of any jump.

3 The 'keeper catches the ball over the player in red, with his hands positioned on the back of the ball and his fingers spread wide. He should now grasp the ball to his chest.

POSITIONING

When faced with an attacker bearing down on goal, 'keepers must make sure that they position themselves effectively, narrowing any shooting angle to make life hard for their opponent. The experts say that goalkeepers should constantly move around to maintain a position in the middle of the goal in relation to the position of the ball. The theory is that an attacking player should never have more than half the goal to aim a shot at. However, when the attacking player is approaching from a wider position, the near post invariably becomes a vulnerable area, and goalkeepers should be encouraged to shuffle across and cover the post.

COMING OFF THE LINE ↓

A goalkeeper has nothing to lose in a one-versus-one situation as the attacking player has a distinct advantage. The 'keeper's first priority should be to get in line with the ball and close off any vulnerable areas, such as the near post. A decision can then be made on whether to leave the line or stay in position. If the 'keeper decides to leave the goal-line, he or she must move forward purposefully and with confidence, making a big obstacle for the attacking player.

←Goalkeepers should avoid going to ground too early. This player has committed himself prematurely and the attacker has a simple task to chip the ball over him.

←This time the goalkeeper stays on his feet and makes himself 'big'. The attacker is distracted and kicks the ball straight at the advancing keeper.

GOALKEEPERS SHOULD COME OUT IF:

1. The attacker does not have the ball within playing distance.
2. They believe they can reach the ball first.

GOALKEEPERS SHOULD STAY PUT IF:

1. The attacker is about to let fly with a shot.
2. The attacker has a supporting team-mate and could, therefore, pass his way around the 'keeper.

WALL WORK→

This simple exercise, which can be practised by players on their own, is an excellent way for goalkeepers to improve their handling skills. The player simply lies on the floor, throws a ball against the wall and dives to save the ball as it rebounds. Players should try to speed up as they get more confident, throwing the ball harder each time. They should also vary the angle so that the ball's movements are less predictable.

DRILL DETAIL
- Player lies in front of a brick wall (which does not have any windows).
- Ball is bounced against the wall and caught as it rebounds.

PROGRESSION
1. Speed and angle can be varied to increase the difficulty of this exercise.

In the past, goalkeeper training involved hitting a few crosses and shots at the 'keeper after he or she had spent an hour or so running around a field. Thankfully, today's 'keepers receive special training to improve their reactions, handling and judgement.

PRACTICE DRILLS

ON THE SPOT →

This exercise helps to improve both reactions and speed off the line. Five balls are spaced in an arc around the six-yard box and each ball is numbered (for younger children coloured discs can be used to replace numbered balls). The coach then stands on the penalty spot and throws balls at the 'keeper to save. At any point during the exercise (and without warning) the coach shouts out a number and the 'keeper must dive onto the corresponding ball. The coach resumes throwing balls from the penalty spot immediately.

DRILL DETAIL

• Balls are spaced around the six-yard box in an arc and numbered.
• The coach throws a ball at the 'keeper from a position around the penalty spot.
• The 'keeper catches the ball and, as he returns it, the coach shouts out the number of one of the balls on the ground, which the 'keeper must now dive upon.

PROGRESSION

1. Speed of throws can be increased to make this exercise progressively more difficult.

PLYOMETRICS ON BENCHES

Quick reactions are essential to goalkeepers, so plyometric exercises should form a significant part of their training. A simple but effective exercise can be performed using two benches laid side by side. Each player hops from foot to foot in a zig-zag pattern across the two benches.

DISTRIBUTION

A long kick downfield used to be the preferred way for goalkeepers to 'distribute' the ball, but in the modern game a more subtle touch is required. The introduction of a new rule in the early 1990s, which banned goalkeepers from picking up the ball after a deliberate backpass, has meant that 'keepers can no longer get away with second-rate ball skills. Today, goalies must be sufficiently skilful to play the ball with either foot when under pressure from opponents. Many coaches also demand that their 'keeper uses the ball effectively and rapidly, delivering accurate and quick throws and kicks to help maintain possession.

1 The ball is held in both hands and dropped from waist height in front of the body.

2 The player keeps his head still and eyes focussed on the ball.

3 A full swing of the leg is made, with the instep making contact with the bottom half of the ball.

4 As the 'keeper follows through, the ball ascends. The head remains still throughout.

KICKING FROM THE HANDS ↑

When clearing a ball that has been caught, goalkeepers can kick from the hands. This technique offers an effective method of clearing the ball over great distances. However, it is often difficult to control the accuracy of the kick.

DEAD-BALL KICKING

Goalkicks can be taken by any player, although ideally goalkeepers should take them, as otherwise attackers are played onside if the ball is played directly forward. The ball is played with the instep using the strike technique demonstrated on page 44.

THROWING ↓

If accuracy rather than distance is required, throwing the ball is the preferred option. Top goalkeepers practise their throwing as much as their kicking, and junior players should do likewise. A quick throw can often be an effective way to set up a counter-attack.

1 The leading leg is placed forward and the ball is brought back to shoulder height.

2 The palm of the throwing hand is placed behind the ball and the body positioned sideways-on to the target. The non-throwing arm points at the target.

3 The ball is released at head height and propelled forward as the throwing arm extends.

ROLLING THE BALL ↓

Setting the ball at the feet of an advancing team-mate can be an excellent way to build from the back, but it is frequently a skill that is ignored by coaches. In theory, it should not be difficult to roll a ball into the path of a colleague, but unless goalkeepers practise their technique, they will find it difficult to judge both the angle and weight of their pass.

1 The goalkeeper (in white) is receiving one-on-one tuition from his coach. Both hands are placed on the ball, with the non-throwing hand on top.

2 The ball is held in the palm of the hand and brought back to hip height. The leading foot (the left for a right-handed throw) is placed well forward and aligned to the target.

3 The ball is released low to the ground as the arm comes through in line with the front foot. Players should try to swing the throwing arm through smoothly to avoid bouncing the ball onto the turf.

SET PICES

6

A successful and well-rehearsed set piece is a sight to behold for a soccer coach. It benefits not only the team on the pitch but also the coach himself, whose reputation is enhanced because of his apparent ability to organize and communicate ideas on the training ground. However, when working with junior players, coaches must forget any thoughts of such glory, focussing instead upon basic techniques and rules rather than any complicated routines.

PASSING THE BALL ↓

Even at junior level, most defending teams anticipate that the ball will be delivered high into the penalty area from a corner. So, by passing it short into the feet of a team-mate, you can benefit from an element of surprise. To be successful, this tactic relies upon the players in the penalty area moving around to create confusion as well as the opportunity for one of them to slip unnoticed towards the kicker. Presuming the pass is successful, the player in possession of the ball should move towards the touchline and pull the ball back from it, as by doing so the defending team cannot push out and catch anybody offside.

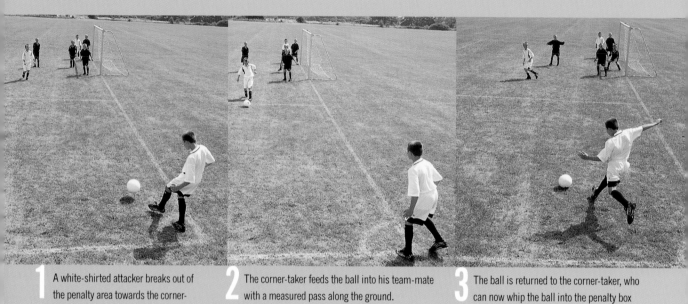

1 A white-shirted attacker breaks out of the penalty area towards the corner-taker.

2 The corner-taker feeds the ball into his team-mate with a measured pass along the ground.

3 The ball is returned to the corner-taker, who can now whip the ball into the penalty box from a different angle.

There are two unique problems that junior coaches must contend with when working on corners. Firstly, not many children are keen on heading the ball, and, secondly, juniors often struggle to kick the ball in the air across the penalty area. To overcome these shortcomings, coaches should work on both heading and striking in separate sessions, but they must be realistic about what their team can achieve from corners. A carefully delivered pass is often the best option for a junior side.

CORNERS

HITTING THE DANGER ZONE ↓

If you are fortunate enough to have both a corner-taker who can strike the ball powerfully and players who can head it effectively, the option of playing the ball high and long becomes realistic. The taker should be encouraged to hit an area midway between the penalty spot and the six-yard line, as this area offers attackers a good chance of hitting the target and puts goalkeepers in a dilemma about whether to stay on the line or come for the cross.

1 A corner-taker who can deliver a ball with both power and control is an asset to any team.

2 The ball arrives in an area that puts the goalkeeper in a dilemma ... should he stay on his line or come for the cross? He decides to stay on his line.

3 A white-shirted attacker is first to the ball and meets the cross with a firm header.

4 The header has too much power for the goalkeeper to keep it out, and the ball nestles in the back of the net.

A VARIED DELIVERY ↓

To be effective from corners, teams must vary their deliveries; playing some balls short into feet while hitting others long to the far post and some to the near post. It is advisable to work out a simple system of hand signals that the corner-taker can use to let team-mates know what he or she plans to do.

A corner played short to a team-mate on the edge of the 18-yard box can often take opposing defenders by surprise.

THROW-INS

The key rules concerning throw-ins have already been explained (see page 27), and all players should be aware of them.

THE DEFENSIVE AND MIDDLE THIRDS

Throw-ins taken in these areas of the field should be directed down the touchline towards the goal you are attacking. Players should not throw the ball in towards the middle of the pitch, as this can result in conceding possession in a potentially dangerous area. The priority is to retain possession, so players must be encouraged to move around to give the thrower targets to aim at.

THE ATTACKING THIRD

In this area of the field, players have the choice of either working the ball down the touchline or throwing it in towards the opposition goal. A long throw directed into the penalty area can cause mayhem, but it should still be directed at a team-mate. Strikers should be reminded that they cannot be offside from a throw-in, so they can surge forward at will. By doing so, they will either offer an option for the thrower or drag a defender out of position and create space for a team-mate.

FREE KICKS

When practising free kicks, many coaches succumb to temptation and overcomplicate matters in search of a clever routine. However, at junior level, free kicks do not need to be decorated with fancy step-overs or dummies, nor do they need to involve four or five players. Quite simply, a free kick should be either a pass or a shot. Speed and accuracy of delivery are all that matter.

THE SHOT →

The bending free kick is both an effective and popular way to get the ball around a defensive wall. The ball is struck with the inside of the foot (as explained on page 61) and for a right-footer moves from right to left. The theory is simple: the player aims the ball wide of the wall and bends it back around and into the corner of the goal.

Some youngsters, however, will struggle to bend the ball with sufficient power and accuracy to beat the 'keeper. As an alternative, such players may prefer to get a team-mate to push the ball to the side of the wall, thus making an angle for them to drive a shot at the unguarded portion of the net.

1 The goalkeeper sets his wall to guard the near post, while he takes care of the other side of the goal.

2 The red team, however, do not attempt to bend the ball around the goal and, instead, the ball is shifted to the side of the wall with a short pass.

KEY RULES

- The ball must be stationary when a free kick is taken – the kick must be taken again if the ball is moving.
- The ball must travel its own circumference before it is considered to be in play. This means that placing a foot on top of the ball does not constitute a free kick being taken.
- Defenders must be 10yds (9.1m) from the ball when a kick is taken.
- Players can be offside from free-kicks.
- Free-kicks awarded to a defending team within its own penalty area can be taken from any other point in the penalty area.

THE PASS →

Junior players should be discouraged from launching the ball aimlessly forward from free kicks. It may be effective for some senior teams to send high free kicks into opposition territory from deep positions, but it is not recommended that youngsters employ this tactic. Instead, they should aim to put the ball down, look up and pass it to the feet of a team-mate. Ideally the pass should be made quickly and decisively, and if possible the ball should go forwards rather than backwards.

ASSESSING THE SITUATION

When the referee awards a free kick, players must immediately check two things. Firstly, they need to check if the kick has been awarded as a direct or indirect kick (see page 24-5), and, secondly, they must assess whether they are close enough to goal to take a shot. Players must be encouraged to be realistic when assessing whether they can shoot for goal or not, as there is little point in a 10-year-old hitting a free kick from 30m (32yds) and watching it dribble towards the goalkeeper's feet. If the kick is not close enough to goal to warrant a shot, the ball should be put down and quickly passed to the feet of a team-mate.

PRACTICE, PRACTICE, PRACTICE

Players will only improve their free-kick technique if they are willing to put in extra time on the practice ground. Organized group sessions offer the chance for players to practise their kicks against a goalkeeper and a defensive wall, but by practising on their own, players can work more intensely on their kicks.

3 Number 9 runs onto the ball and, before any defenders can react, crashes a shot at goal.

4 By moving the ball to the side of the wall, the attacking team gives number 9 a greater area of the goal to aim at.

5 The 'keeper scurries across his line, but there is nothing he can do to keep the ball from finishing in the back of the net.

1 The player on the left does the sensible thing here. With the goal out of range, he picks up the ball and puts it down ready for the free kick.

2 He plays a simple, short pass to his nearby team-mate, who can now carry the ball forward.

3 No risks were taken and, while no glory was achieved, the blue team retains possession and begins to move forward again.

PENALTIES

Everybody likes practising penalties, but when it comes to the real thing, volunteers are not always as forthcoming. Coaches should remember that the best players do not necessarily make the best penalty-takers. The basic skill of beating a goalkeeper from 12yds (10.9m) is not difficult, but in the context of a highly competitive football match it can be daunting. And, with the introduction of penalty shoot-outs to settle many competitions nowadays, there are more and more of these nerve-tingling scenarios, even at junior level.

PRACTISING PENALTIES

Traditionalists believe there is no point practising penalties because you cannot replicate the tension of a match on a training ground. However, while this is true, it is important for players to hone their technique in practice sessions so that they are confident in their ability to hit the target should they be called upon to take a spot-kick during a match.

By placing cones in the corners of the goal, players can practise their penalty technique without the need for a goalkeeper.

POWER OR PLACEMENT

Junior players should be encouraged to aim their penalties rather than blast them. A shot placed in the corner is impossible for a 'keeper to reach, but one blasted straight down the middle of the goal relies on the goalie getting out of the way. There is also a greater risk of missing the target altogether when going for power over placement. As with any shooting practice, it may be helpful to place cones in the corners of the goal so that players can focus their efforts.

GOOD PENALTY ↓

A carefully struck penalty directed hard and low towards the corner of the goal is destined for the net.

BAD PENALTY ↓

This time, however, the player leans back and strikes a hopeful shot over the centre of the crossbar.

PENALTY TIPS

1. Never change your mind on the run up. Decide what you are going to do and stick to the plan.
2. Look at the goal before you take the kick, but look at the ball when striking.
3. Keep your head down to avoid skying the ball.

TACTICAL PLAY

7

Talent, skill and fitness are all important, but for a soccer team to fulfil its potential it must be more than a mere collection of individuals.
In short, the 'whole' must be more than the sum of its parts.
Cooperation, organization and discipline are all required, and it is the job of the coach to foster these qualities in junior players.

DEFENSIVE PRINCIPLES

At junior level, the art of defending is not about winning last-ditch tackles or making telepathic interceptions. Instead, it is about working as a team to win back possession by applying systematic pressure to the opposition.

DEFENDING AS A TEAM

Gone are the days when centre-forwards and wingers could stand on the halfway line with hands on hips if they lost possession. In the modern game, every player has defensive duties, and the team must work as a unit to win back the ball. Coaches should take time before every game to make it clear to each player which of the opposition team they are responsible for in any given situation.

All soccer players, whatever their position, need to appreciate what the coach expects of them. Junior players, however, should not be pigeonholed too soon, and you should be willing to try them in different positions before deciding where they are best deployed. For this reason, it is a good idea to involve all players in every training session.

TACKLING

It is inadvisable to spend a great deal of time practising block tackles or sliding tackles for two reasons. Firstly, there is a significant risk of players getting injured, and, secondly, junior players should be encouraged to close down and force the opposition into errors rather than dive into tackles. Junior players will often over-commit themselves when trying to make a tackle, thus giving their opponent the chance to go round them. Instead, players should direct opponents away from danger and towards covering team-mates.

DEFENDING AS A TEAM

MARKING SIZE FOR SIZE

When marking opponents at a set piece, players should be encouraged to mark 'size for size'. This means that defenders should mark attackers who are a similar size rather than continuing to take responsibility for the player they are looking after in open play. Players should stand near to their opponent, but not so close that it is easy for him or her to roll them.

CLOSING DOWN AND COVERING →

There is no surer way to confuse a junior player than to stand on the touchline barking out jargon-filled instructions. A particular favourite for many coaches is the phrase 'close down'. It is, however, pointless using such soccer shorthand unless you have first taken the time to explain exactly what you mean on the training ground. A small-sided practice game is ideal for teaching youngsters the principles of closing down. All you need do is let the game flow until an attacker has the ball in the final third of the field but finds the path to goal blocked. If you stop the game now, you can explain how you want your defender to combat the opposition's attacking threat.

THE THEORY

When faced with an attacking team moving forward, your team must know exactly what is expected of them. The aim is to make the play compact, halving the pitch and concentrating all defensive effort accordingly. For the system to work, every player should have a job:

1. CLOSING DOWN

The defender nearest the ball should apply direct pressure to the player with the ball in an effort to force an error. The defender should stand on the balls of his or her feet, side-on to the opponent and with eyes fixed on the ball. The aim is to direct the attacker in towards fellow defenders, who may be able to win the ball. This is done by standing outside the line of the attacker's run.

2. FIRST COVER

The second-nearest player moves round on the cover to act as an insurance policy in case the attacker gets past the first defender. The cover defender should take up a position on an imaginary line between the ball and the centre of the goal.

3. REMAINING COVER

Any remaining defenders should shuffle across the pitch to occupy the half of the pitch that is currently under attack.

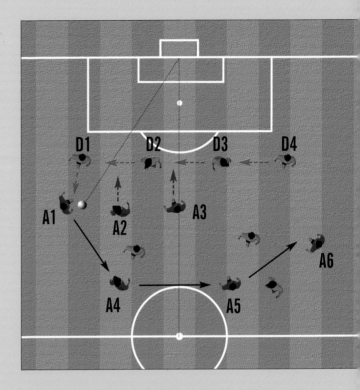

The red team defends perfectly to see off a blue attack. As the move progresses, the red defenders shuffle across the pitch, providing cover and applying pressure to the opponent in possession. The effect is that the pitch is 'halved' with all four defenders concentrated in the active area of the pitch. At the start of the attacking team's move, A1 has the ball on the edge of the penalty area. D1 moves toward A1 and closes him down. D2, in turn, moves to his right to offer cover and positions himself in a line directly between the ball and the centre of the goal. D3 and D4 also move across and keep a watchful eye on A2 and A3. With no other option, A1 has to turn away from goal and pass the ball to A4 who shifts the point of attack to the opposite flank, whereupon the red team will repeat the same routine.

TIP

When faced with an advancing opposition, defenders should try to make the play compact, focussing defensive resources on the half of the pitch under attack. It is better to ignore a player out wide on the far side of the pitch than to reduce the number of covering players nearer to the action. A far greater threat would be caused by an attacker exploiting space through the middle of the pitch than out wide.

INSIDE OR OUT?

There is much debate about whether to 'show' attacking players inside (i.e. in towards goal) or outside (down the wings). The consensus now is that the safest route is to show opponents in toward covering team-mates. If a defender does not have the benefits of any cover players, it is advisable to guide the attacker away from goal and down the flank.

THE SAFE ROUTE INSIDE→

1 The white-shirted attacker has his path to goal blocked by a defender.

THE RISKY PATH OUTSIDE→

1 This time, the blue-shirted defender offers his opponent space on the outside.

2 The defender positions himself just outside the line of the ball, and the attacker is guided in towards goal and also towards a covering defender.

3 The first defender holds his position, forcing the attacker to run across the pitch and the covering player nips in to win the ball.

2 The attacker moves forward into the space, where there are no covering defenders, and whips in a cross.

3 A second attacker collects the ball and is now in possession in a dangerous position in the penalty area.

1

2

3

4

PASS AND MOVE

Passing a football to a team-mate should be a simple enough task, but for some junior players it seems to be the hardest thing in the world. Dribbling, juggling, shooting . . . 'no problem, coach!', but ask them to lay the ball off to a colleague rather than take on a defender, and you can expect some old-fashioned looks from your young players. However, as a coach or parent, it is your job to teach your soccer prodigies the value of simple pass-and-move tactics, while also explaining that they do not always have to jink their way around three defenders to be a good player.

← THE WALL PASS

Contrary to what most young players believe, a burst of pace and a drop of the shoulder is not necessarily the most effective way to get past an opponent. A safer and far more straightforward option is the wall pass (also called the one-two or the give-and-go).

1 The blue-shirted attacker has his path to goal blocked by a defender on the edge of the 18-yard box. With the goal in such close proximity, the attacker contemplates taking on his opponent.

2 He resists the temptation to drive forward and, instead, plays the ball into the feet of his team-mate on the left. Once he has played the ball, rather than stand and admire his pass, he makes a forward run past the defender. It is this run that is the key to the success of the wall pass. Communication is also important, and players should give a shout of 'give and go' as they pass the ball so that their team-mates know their intention.

3 The second attacker plays an angled pass into the path of his on-running team-mate. The ball must be played away from any defenders and should be rolled along the ground.

4 The blue-shirted attacker runs onto the ball and bears down on goal, while the defender is left trailing in his wake.

PRACTICE DRILL — PASS AND MOVE ↓

When junior players makes a successful pass, their instinctive reaction is to stand back and admire the quality of the delivery. But, as all good coaches know, there is no excuse for standing still during a match. Once a player has passed the ball, his first thought should be to get into a position from where he can receive the ball back again. Put simply, junior players must learn to pass and move, and the following drill should help make running off the ball become a habit.

DRILL DETAIL

- Space a group of players equidistantly around a circle that is 20m (22yds) in diameter.
- Set a boundary of cones around the outside the circle to prevent the players from extending it and making the exercise easier.
- Get players to pass the ball across the circle and into the feet of a colleague.
- As the ball is received, the player who passed it follows the ball's path, running across the circle to take the place of his team-mate, who, in turn, passes the ball and moves off after it.
- This exercise should be practised regularly, though its duration should never exceed ten minutes.

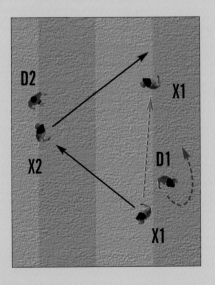

The attacking team (the Xs) have their path forward blocked by defenders, who appear to have their opponents well marked. However, X1 passes the ball to X2, who returns the ball into X1's path. Defender 1 now has to turn and chase, handing the initiative to the attacking side and X1, who breaks forward in possession of the ball.

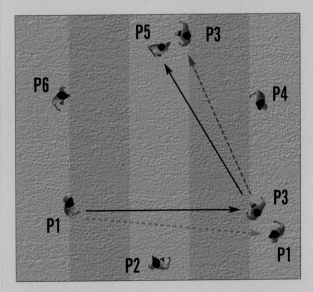

P1 passes to P3 and then follows the ball, taking the place of P3 in the circle. P3 in turn passes the ball to P5 and then takes his or her place. And so the drill continues.

SETTING THE BALL

The centre-forward has traditionally been regarded as the player who finishes off an attacking move, coming into the play at the final moment to carry out the critical act of putting the ball into the net. However, in the modern game, strikers do much more, and in a good, passing team they should play a pivotal role in setting up attacks. By 'setting' or 'bouncing' the ball off the centre forward, your team will simultaneously move forwards and open up a range of attacking options.

THE UNSELFISH OPTION ↓

When the ball is played into the feet of a striker on the edge of the box, his first thought will be to try and turn his marker and fire in a shot at goal. If, however, he controls the ball and sets it back to the midfielder, who had played the original pass, he will set up a better shooting chance.

1 The red team's number 9 is in possession and surges out of midfield.

2 Number 9 plays the ball into the feet of his team-mate, the centre-forward, who gets in position to shield the ball from the white-shirted defender.

3 The centre-forward controls the ball and, using a sidefoot technique, pushes it into the path of his oncoming team-mate.

4 The number 9 runs onto the ball and drives it towards goal.

A VARIETY OF OPTIONS

A ball played into the feet of a centre-forward can give an attacking team a variety of options, although only if the supporting players make quick and decisive runs off the ball.

OPTION 1: The centre-forward returns the ball to the onrushing midfielder, who shoots for goal (see photographs).

OPTION 2: The centre-forward returns the ball to the midfielder, and then turns and spins back towards goal. The midfielder can then push the ball forward into the path of the centre-forward, who has now moved beyond his marker.

OPTION 3: One of the most effective and simple tactics is for the centre-forward to receive the ball and then knock it out wide to a third player, who can then build an attack down the wing. The centre-forward, in turn, moves forward in anticipation of a cross once the ball has been worked out to the flank.

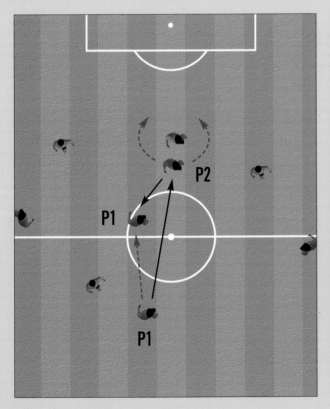

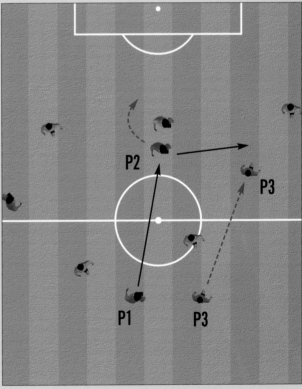

The blue team are attacking the goal at the top of this illustration, and they have possession with P1. The ball is passed into the feet of P2 (the centre-forward), who 'sets the ball', laying it back into the path of the onrushing P1. As P1 collects the return pass, P2 has the option of spinning into space on either side of his marker. He is now available for a pass while simultaneously opening up space by taking his marker away from the middle of the pitch.

The blue team are once more in possession with P1, who again passes the ball into the centre-forward (P2). This time, however, P2 simply controls the ball and pushes a pass into the path of P3, who is moving forward down the right wing. P2 then spins off to the left to get in position for a cross or a return pass.

SMALL-SIDED FORMATIONS

At junior level many competitive leagues play small-sided games, usually eight-a-side. It is felt that younger players benefit from the fact that they each enjoy a greater share of possession than if they played a full 11-a-side game. Another factor is that younger children often struggle to cope with the additional physical exertions of playing on a full-size pitch, while many of them are also unable to kick the ball with sufficient power to make any headway.

FORMATIONS

It is easy for coaches to get unnecessarily preoccupied with systems of play, tactics and formations, but it is vital to remember that young players will neither be capable nor interested in remembering a long list of complex instructions during a game. At junior level, good tactics are simple tactics. It is important, however, to employ a formation that suits the abilities and ambitions of your team.

MOVE PLAYERS AROUND

Some young players are keen to embrace labels, and seem desperate to pigeonhole themselves as 'right-backs' or 'central midfielders' at the earliest opportunity. However, a nine- or ten-year-old cannot possibly know what their best position is yet. At junior level, it is important that coaches encourage individuals to try out different positions so that they can find out where their strengths and weaknesses lie.

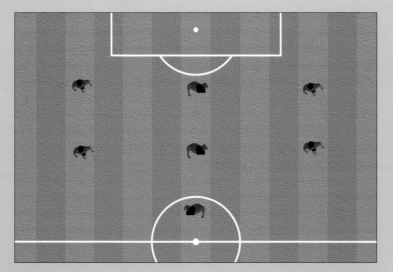

← 3-3-1

This is the standard formation for an eight-a-side team. A bank of three defenders is protected by three midfielders, who simultaneously support a lone striker. The system works in a similar way to 11-a-side's popular 4-4-2 formation. For 3-3-1 to work effectively, however, it is vital that the centre-forward plays a pivotal role, setting the ball for his team-mates. Since the striker plays alone, there is little point in him trying to turn his marker as he will easily be outnumbered by supporting players. It is far better to knock the ball back towards the midfield and await reinforcements.

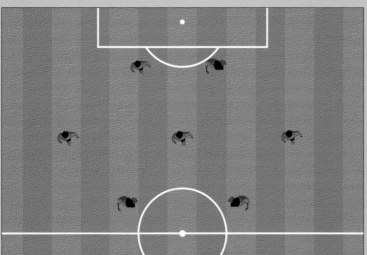

← 2-3-2

The 2-3-2 system is an attacking formation which relies upon midfield players to take full responsibility in defensive situations. With only two dedicated defenders, the two wide midfield players usually have to operate as part-time wing-backs, shuffling across when needed. Similarly, the second striker must also be willing to tuck into midfield if his team-mates get outnumbered. Flexibility, therefore, is the key to this system.

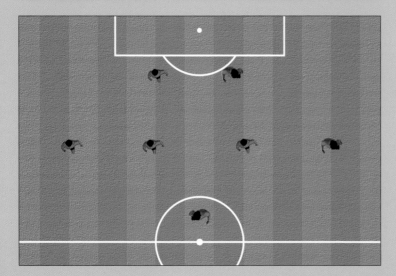

← 2-4-1

The 2-4-1 formation can be both an attacking and a defensive system, depending on how high up the field the two wide midfielders operate. If they tuck in alongside the central midfielders and play a conservative game, the 2-4-1 is a solid system with the emphasis on defence. If, however, the widemen play like wingers, getting up alongside the centre-forward whenever possible, then the formation becomes a far more attacking one.

Once junior teams begin to compete on full-sized pitches, games become 11-a-side and coaches have to learn a whole new catalogue of tactical systems. This time, however, the formations all have familiar names and are already employed by the big professional teams and managers.

SIMPLE INSTRUCTIONS ARE BEST

When preparing a team for a match, players will invariably switch off if team-talks become too long or too boring. Simple directions given to each player one at a time are the most effective way to get your team following orders out on the pitch on a match day.

4-4-2 AND 4-2-4 →

The most popular formation in world football is the tried-and-trusted 4-4-2 system that came to prominence during the 1960s. It was the system with which Brazil's famous team of 1970 – still widely regarded as the greatest team of all time – won the World Cup, and it is also the formation employed by successful club sides like Machester United and Bayern Munich.

The foundation of a good 4-4-2 system is a solid defence. The two central defenders are flanked by two full-backs (a left-back and a right-back). The full-backs play an important attacking role but should not both go forward at the same time; if they did, the two centre-backs would be left exposed to a counter-attack. If one of the full-backs pushes into a forward position, the opposite full-back should tuck in to support the other defenders, effectively giving the team a back-three. The raiding full-back supports a midfield that already boasts four players, so the traditional 4-4-2 has now become a more modern 3-5-2. From this example you can see how different tactics can overlap depending on circumstances.

Similarly, the second bank of four players – the midfield – can also switch shape to affect a change of formation. By pushing forward into advanced positions, almost up alongside the central strikers, the two wide midfielders can operate as orthodox wingers. It is a tactic that is often used by teams who are chasing a game and trying to score a goal at all costs.

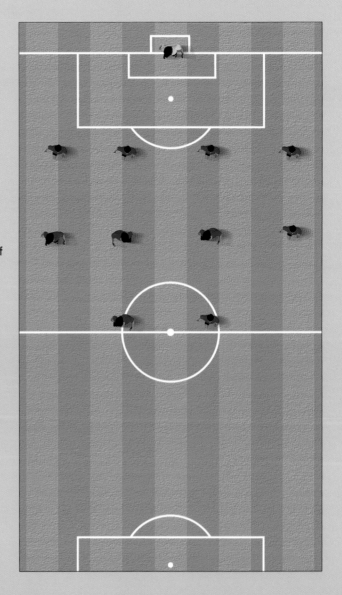

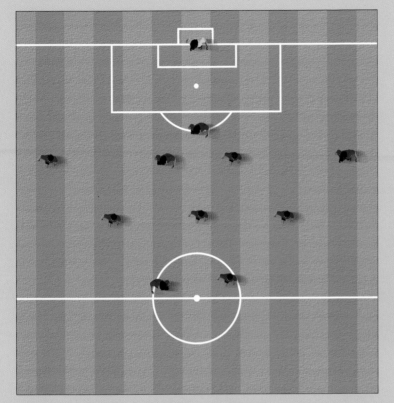

← 3-5-2 OR 5-3-2

The 3-5-2 system has been popular in much of Europe for more than 20 years. It offers defensive security through the sweeper or third centre-back, and flexibility, since it can be both a defensive system (5-3-2) and an attacking solution too (3-5-2). Most coaches regard this system as one that is fundamentally defensive, but, in truth, it is as attacking as the players and coach want it to be. In many cases, if teams are happy to attack from a solid base and use wingbacks, a 5-3-2 system quickly evolves into 3-5-2.

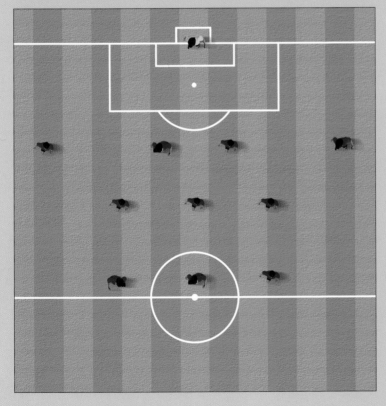

← 4-3-3

The 4-3-3 formation is rarely used today, although it has been employed by some clubs in recent times, including Leeds United in the English Premier League. Under this system, the full-backs are expected to provide both attacking width and defensive cover. A two-man central defence is also employed, thus providing cover for the marauding full-backs. In midfield and attack the 4-3-3 formation is made up of two banks of three. However, the attacking and defensive responsibilities of these players varies tremendously according to the ideas of individual coaches.

Small-sided games provide an effective and flexible framework for coaches to teach junior players a variety of techniques, from first touch to closing down. They can also be used to teach players tactical responsibilities and the importance of team play.

GAME WITHOUT GOALS →

Getting junior players to pass the ball is not an easy task, but this training drill should encourage even the most greedy of centre forwards to pass to a team-mate. A pitch is marked out using cones (as illustrated), but there are no goals. The idea is that by removing the goals then players are left free to concentrate on their passing unfettered by the temptation to dribble past opponents and shoot at goal. Points are awarded for three consecutive successful passes. As players get more proficient, the number of passes can be increased. This drill demonstrates the importance of moving off the ball and retaining possession.

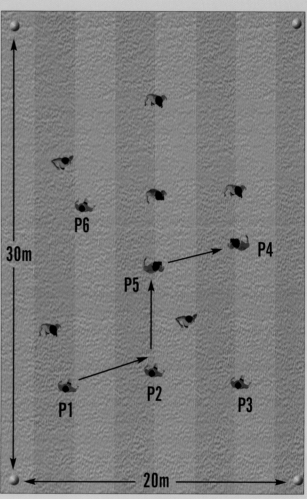

The blue team scores a point by completing three consecutive passes (from P1 to P2 to P5 and on to P4).

SMALL-SIDED GAMES

STOP BALL ↓

An alternative possession game can be played with only minor modifications to the pitch used for the 'game without goals'.

1. By setting a gate of two cones spaced 1m (3ft 4ins) apart at each end of the pitch, players can focus on moving the ball forwards rather than merely on retaining possession.

2. The objective is now to stop the ball on the line between the two cones to score a 'goal'.

KEEP IT SIMPLE

A keep-ball session, (see page 46) in which players are restricted to a set number of touches, usually two, is a simple but effective way to teach junior players the key skills of possession football.

111

INNOVATION AND OBSERVATION

There are countless different small-sided drills with infinite variations and numerous names, but there is still room for you to innovate. Do not be afraid to change things around or to adapt a recognized drill to meet your needs.

You should also be prepared to stop a small-sided game to highlight examples of both good and bad play. If, for example, your drill is intended to encourage players to use the width of the pitch, but they are bunched around the ball, you should blow your whistle and ask the players to stop where they are so that you can point out the error of their ways. You should always observe small-sided games, just as you would any training drill, taking time to encourage good play and correct any faults.

CONDITIONED GAMES →

A conditioned game can help players think about their positioning and their role within the team. In the example illustrated, the pace of the game is restricted by the use of three zones (defence, midfield and attack). Two players from each team are positioned in each zone, and the defenders and attackers must never leave their respective zones. Midfielders, meanwhile, can move between zones, fetching and carrying the ball for their team-mates. In theory, the defenders focus on the job of marking the opposing team's attackers, who in turn try to find space in a restricted area. The midfielders must try to retain concentration and cover the forward runs of their counterparts.

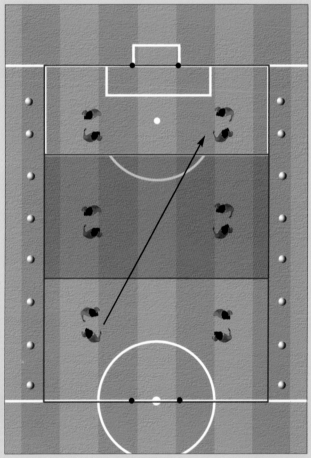

In this moderate-intensity conditioned game, players are restricted to particular areas to limit their exertion while tackling is not allowed in the middle third of the pitch. Passes are allowed between any zones (as illustrated) and balls are ready on the sidelines to keep the game running.

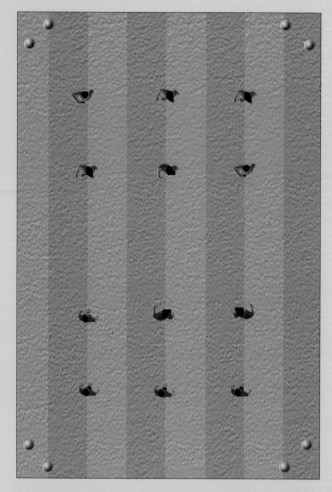

← GAME WITH FOUR GOALS

A game with four goals may sound confusing, but it should help improve positional sense and ensure that players begin to use the whole pitch. Each goal is made up of a gate of two cones spaced 1m (3ft 4ins) apart positioned appoximately 2m (6ft 8ins) inside the corner of the pitch. To score goals, players must pass the ball between the two cones, but the ball must not leave the playing area. Play is continuous but consecutive goals cannot be scored in the same corner. As a result, players must switch the play from one side of the pitch to the other, thereby encouraging them to stay out wide and in their positions.

1 Take the time to clearly explain this drill, as this coach is doing. Players often get confused because they cannot score consecutive goals in the same corner.

2 As the red-shirted team score in the right-hand goal, one of their team-mates has already moved into position in the opposite corner, ready for when play is switched.

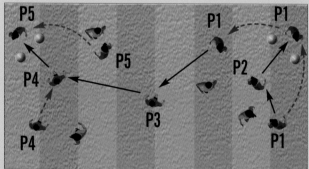

The top diagram shows the pitch layout for the game with four goals, while the lower illustration depicts the blue team scoring two consecutive goals in opposite corners. P1 passes to P2 and then moves round the back of the goal himself. P2 scores by shooting between the two cones and P1 collects the ball, carrying it a short distance before passing to P3. With the ball in the middle of the pitch, P4 moves into position and receives a pass from P3. Meanwhile, P5 has moved around the back of the goal to await P4's shot.

SPEED AND AGILITY

Children usually have a good standard of general fitness, so at junior level coaches should not have to spend time working on stamina and endurance exercises. However, it is still important to tailor players' fitness to meet the game's requirements. A few simple exercises can do wonders for physical conditioning for soccer, and the key areas of speed and agility should be the primary focus of any training drill.

FAST FEET

STATIC PRACTICE ↓

Placing each foot on top of a static ball looks simple, but it is not quite as easy as it first appears.
The objective is to keep the ball still while touching it gently with the sole of each foot. This exercise will help improve a player's coordination and control as well as his or her speed of foot.

1 Two cones define the line upon which the ball is set. The player must aim to keep the ball in the centre of the line.

2 The player extends both arms to aid balance as he removes his right foot and prepares to place the sole of his left shoe on top of the ball.

3 The ball has moved slightly and the player has to adjust his position as he prepares to put his left foot down.

SIDE TO SIDE ↓

This exercise is essentially a variation of the static practice illustrated above.
The player must try to move the ball, in a controlled fashion, between the inside of each boot.

1 Boundary cones are used once more to define the player's position. He stands lightly with his weight on the balls of his feet, and prepares to make contact.

2 The ball is struck sharply with the inside of the left foot and, as before, the arms are extended to aid balance.

3 The player takes his second touch, clipping the ball back with his right foot.

TOE TAPS

A player with fast feet can manipulate the ball quickly within confined areas and, as a result, has a distinct advantage over more ponderous opponents. Fast feet will enable him to nick the ball away from defenders and move it sharply out of trouble. Opponents can also be sucked in by a swift change of direction or a subtle drag back. Toe taps offer an excellent and enjoyable way for players to improve the speed of their footwork.

POINT TO POINT ↓

Once players are confident moving their feet quickly around a static ball, they can progress onto exercises that involve lateral or linear movement. The drill illustrated here shows a player moving the ball along a line while all the time facing forwards. It is an exercise that will improve not only footwork, but also balance and control.

1 Cones are used to define the line along which the player must move. He must remain adjacent to the ball and at right angles to the direction of travel.

2 The player rolls his right foot over the ball to move it in a controlled fashion along the line.

3 The player has successfully moved the ball from left to right, and he takes a final touch to complete the movement from cone to cone.

BACK AND FORTH↓

Moving the ball forward and back using only the soles of the feet is a difficult skill that requires both coordination and fast feet. Players should be encouraged to use both feet and should move back and forth to a mark no more than 20m (22yds) ahead of them.

1 Starting between two cones, the player puts his right foot on top of the ball and pushes it forwards.

2 With his arms used for balance and his body positioned upright, the player picks his knees up high and rolls his foot over the ball.

3 The player reaches the end of his forward run, but instead of turning, he begins to roll the ball backwards to his starting point.

MOVEMENT AND CONTROL

FAST-FOOT LADDERS

The drills illustrated here are intended to promote the importance of maintaining balance and control while moving at speed over short distances. Ordinary garden canes can be used instead of the fast-foot ladders shown in the photographs, but care must be taken to space them properly. Intervals of 45cm (18ins) are recommended.

LOOK STRAIGHT AHEAD ↓

This exercise is an extension of the cane drill illustrated on page 19. Players must move through the ladder or canes as normal, but to encourage them to look up, the coach stands at the end of the line and throws a ball for them to head or catch. There are many variations of this exercise, and coaches should experiment to meet the aims of a particular session. Double steps, in which both feet are placed one at a time in each space on the ladder, are particularly useful for developing quick feet.

1 The player moves through the ladder with a good running style, bringing her knees up high as she moves forward.

2 To encourage the player to look up rather than at her feet, the coach stands at the end of the line and throws a ball to her.

3 The player heads the ball back towards the coach and moves back to the start of the exercise.

SIDESTEPPING LADDER WORK ↓

Footballers are often required to sidestep their way forwards during matches, and this exercise will help them practise the movement while working on their balance, coordination and speed of foot. Players must place each foot – one at a time – inside each gap on the ladder.

1 The player stands lightly on the balls of his feet and springs between the gaps in the ladder. The right foot leads.

2 The left foot is brought down beside the right, in the same gap on the ladder.

3 With his arms out to maximize his balance, the player continues his run with his right foot leading the way.

BALL WATCHING ON THE LADDER ↓

Players instinctively look at their feet when making their way down the fast-foot ladder, but during a match they will need to direct their eyes at the ball and their opponents rather than their footwear. To break this habit, the following drill, in which players sidestep down the ladder while exchanging chest passes with the coach, should be employed.

1 The player moves down the ladder, while the coach travels alongside.

2 The coach throws the ball toward the player, who is forced to look up as he prepares to catch the ball.

3 Without breaking stride or looking down, the player catches the ball, returns it to the coach and continues his run down the ladder.

EXPLOSIVE POWER

HURDLES

Exercises that are intended to improve a player's reactions and acceleration are often called plyometrics. This type of training should be done regularly, though only for short periods, usually between five and ten minutes. An extended plyometric session can lead to injury and fatigue.

SPRING OVER THE HURDLES ↓

All players, from goalkeepers to centre forwards, will benefit from this simple exercise that is intended to improve both reactions and jumping ability. By springing over closely spaced, small hurdles, players move rapidly through the obstacles. Players should be encouraged to surge up quickly after each landing, rather than sinking to a low squat before ascending again. Each player should do no more than five repetitions of this exercise in one session.

1 The player bounds over a short hurdle, lifting both knees high above the obstacle.

2 Both feet make contact with the ground on landing, but the player does not sink to a low squat but, instead, bounds sharply up again.

3 She 'explodes' into another jump over the next hurdle. The movement through the hurdles is continuous, rather than a series of distinct jumps.

ONE FOOT AT A TIME ↓

A conventional hurdling style, in which one foot leads and one follows, can be used to work on both reactions and coordination. With the hurdles still spaced closely, the player must explode over the obstacles, but greater control is needed than with the technique used to spring over them.

1 There is not sufficient room for the player to take each hurdle in his stride, so instead he must bound over them from virtually a standing start each time.

2 The left leg leads and the right leg follows as the player prepares to land between two hurdles.

3 As soon as the player clears one hurdle, he prepares to bound over the next. As with the spring technique, players should be encouraged to surge up quickly after each landing.

SIDESTEPPING THROUGH HURDLES ↓

By springing over closely spaced hurdles using a side-on motion, players can improve both their coordination and their plyometric fitness. As with the other hurdling exercises, players should be encouraged to spring up quickly between hurdles. Repetitions should also be limited to a maximum of five per session.

1 The right leg leads as the player drives over each hurdle.

2 Both arms are extended to improve balance as the player strides this hurdle.

3 The left leg is brought over sharply to join the right, before the next hurdle is crossed.

REACTION AND COORDINATION

HOPSCOTCH

Players of all ages and abilities can benefit from a game of hopscotch. The pattern of jumping and hopping is perfect for older players to work on their plyometric fitness, while for younger footballers, simply placing their feet in the hoops helps them improve their coordination. If striving to improve plyometric fitness, players must be encouraged to exaggerate the spring between each hoop.

1 Players form an orderly queue behind the two small cones, as the player in white hops into the first red hoop and bounds forward.

2 With one foot in each of the second row of red hoops, the player prepares to hop onto her right foot and into the first yellow hoop.

3+4 The player repeats the pattern of hops and jumps as she moves through to the end of the course. The coach, meanwhile, looks on and encourages the players to progress through the obstacles at a swift pace.

HOOPS

The old-fashioned hoop is an extremely useful tool for the soccer coach. By simply bounding between them, players can work on their explosive fitness, and by moving in and out of them in a predetermined pattern, reactions and coordination are also improved.

DOUBLE-STEPPING THROUGH THE HOOPS

This exercise uses a similar pattern of hoops as hopscotch, but, instead of working on plyometric fitness, it promotes both fast feet and coordination. Players have to put each foot, one at a time, in each of the hoops and are forced to switch direction sharply as they move through the course.

1 The right foot leads as the player moves from the first hoop onto the next.

2 With both feet in the right-hand red hoop, the player must now switch direction and move towards the single yellow hoop.

3 By shifting his weight onto his left side, the player swings sharply into the first yellow hoop. This time it is his left foot that leads.

4 The right foot is brought alongside the left in the first yellow hoop. The circuit is completed by repeating the sequence of movements that was used to get through the red hoops. Young players need to be reminded to concentrate and go slowly so that they don't tread on any of the hoops – as is the case here.

GLOSSARY

Blades
A type of soccer boot that has cleats on the sole, rather like a baseball boot. A relatively new innovation in soccer.

Calf
Area of the leg, found at the back of the shin. A term usually used to refer to the muscle found in this position.

Closing down
Defensive technique used to deny opponents time and space.

Conditioned game
Small-sided game in which players' movements are restricted by boundaries to limit their exertions.

Cruyff turn
An attacking move first used by Holland's legendary forward Johan Cruyff.

Diuretic
Substances which cause increased output of urine. Diuretics should never be consumed at half-time. Coffee, tea and alcohol are all diuretics.

Dynamic flex
An approach to warming up that requires players to move around while they stretch rather than work from a static position.

Groin
Muscles on the inside of the thigh, which are frequently strained by soccer players in the act of stretching or kicking.

Hamstring
A muscle group located at the back of the leg, and which stretches from the lower buttock to the back of the knee.

Isotonic drinks
Easily absorbed into the blood stream, an isotonic solution provides quick rehydration. A simple isotonic drink can be made by mixing fruit juice and water in equal measures.

Ligaments

Tough, fibrous tissues which link to the bone and reinforce the joint. Ligaments keep the joints in place while allowing great flexibility. Ligament injuries are common in football. It can take a great deal of time and rest for a ligament to regain its strength and flexibility once damaged.

Overlap

An overlap is a run made off the ball, usually down the wing. The runner makes his run from behind the ball, getting ahead of the ball, which is held by a team-mate; the latter then releases the ball in front of the runner.

Plyometric training

Training which develops explosive power within the muscles. Examples of plyometric training include jumping over hurdles and running across benches.

Scoops

The term used to describe the technique used by goalkeepers to catch crosses and shots played at below chest height. The hands are closed round the ball in a scooping motion as it hits the keeper's chest.

Sweeper

Defensive position which refers to the last player in a central defensive trio. A sweeper usually plays alongside two markers and is responsible for patrolling the area behind his two colleagues. He is also expected to carry the ball out from the back.

Tendons

Tendons are linking agents which join muscles to bone.

The trap

The basic method of controlling a football using the foot.

'Ws'

The 'Ws' are used to deal with shots and crosses played at or above chest height. The hands are placed in front of the body, with fingers spread wide and thumbs touching each other.

Warm-down

A short period of gentle exercise (similar to a warm-up), which should follow every match. This will help to break down any lactate that has built up in the muscles during exercise.

Warm-up

A warm-up should be carried out prior to any exercise. It is intended to raise the heart rate prior to competitive exertion and warm the muscles to make them more supple.

Wing-back

Variation on the full-back position. Wing-backs are usually used in a 3-5-2 or 5-3-2 system. They are responsible for patrolling the flanks and are expected to spend a great deal of the game attacking. However, they must also defend their wing when required, as a result, this is a stamina-sapping position.

INDEX

PICTURE ACKNOWLEDGEMENTS

All photography © **Octopus Publishing Group Limited**
/Mark Newcombe except for the following listed below:
Steve Bacon 7.
Fila (UK) Limited/www.fila.com 23 top, 23 bottom left.
Octopus Publishing Group Limited/Richard Francis 46.
Umbro/www.umbro.com/(Tel: 0161 492 2222) 23 bottom right.